D0005540

THE GOSPELS

INTERPRETING BIBLICAL TEXTS

The Gospels, Fred B. Craddock

New Testament Apocalyptic, Paul S. Minear

The Pentateuch, Lloyd R. Bailey, Sr.

INTERPRETING BIBLICAL TEXTS

The Gospels

Fred B. Craddock

LLOYD R. BAILEY, Sr.
and
VICTOR P. FURNISH, EDITORS

ABINGDON   NASHVILLE

BS2555.2
.C68

0 0694 3474

THE GOSPELS

Copyright © 1981 by Abingdon

Second Printing 1981

All rights reserved.
No part of this book may be reproduced in any manner
whatsoever without written permission of the publisher
except brief quotations embodied in critical articles
or reviews. For information address Abingdon,
Nashville, Tennessee.

Library of Congress Cataloging in Publication Data

CRADDOCK, FRED B
   The Gospels.
   (Interpreting Biblical Texts)
   Bibliography: p.
   1. Bible. N.T. Gospels—Criticism, interpretation, etc.
   I. Title. II. Series.
   BS2555.2.C68   225.6   80-26270

ISBN 0-687-15655-6 (pbk.)

Unless otherwise noted, all Scripture quotations are from the Revised Standard
Version of the Bible, copyrighted 1946, 1952, © 1971, 1973 by the Division of
Christian Education of the National Council of the Churches of Christ in the
U.S.A., and are used by permission.

MANUFACTURED BY THE PARTHENON PRESS AT
NASHVILLE, TENNESSEE, UNITED STATES OF AMERICA

INTERPRETING BIBLICAL TEXTS:
Editors' Foreword

The volumes in this series have been planned for those who are convinced that the Bible has meaning for our life today, and who wish to enhance their skills as interpreters of the biblical texts. Such interpreters must necessarily engage themselves in two closely related tasks: (1) determining as much as possible about the original meaning of the various biblical writings, and (2) determining in what respect these texts are still meaningful today. The objective of the present series is to keep both of these tasks carefully in view, and to provide assistance in relating the one to the other.

Because of this overall objective it would be wrong to regard the individual volumes in this series as commentaries, as homiletical expositions of selected texts, or as abstract discussions of "the hermeneutical problem." Rather, they have been written in order to identify and illustrate what is involved in relating the meaning of the biblical texts in their own times to their meaning in ours. Biblical commentaries and other technical reference works sometimes focus exclusively on the first, paying little or no attention to the second. On the other hand, many attempts to expound the contemporary "relevance" of biblical themes or passages pay scant attention to the intentions of the texts themselves. And although one of the standard topics of "hermeneutics" is how a text's original meaning relates to its present meaning, such discussions often employ highly technical philosophical language and proceed with little reference to concrete examples. By way of contrast, the present volumes are written in language that will be understood by scholars, clergy and laypersons alike, and they deal with concrete texts, actual problems of interpretation, and practical procedures for moving from "then" to "now."

Each contributor to this series is committed to three basic tasks: (1) a description of the salient features of the particular type of biblical literature or section of the canon assigned to him; (2) the identification and explanation of the basic assumptions that guide his analysis and explication of those materials; and (3) the discussion of possible contemporary meanings of representative texts, in view of the specified assumptions with which the interpreter approaches them. Considerations that should be borne in mind by the interpreter in reflecting upon contemporary meanings of these texts are introduced by the sign ● and are accentuated with a different size of type.

The assumptions that are brought to biblical interpretation may vary from one author to the next, and will undoubtedly differ from those of many readers. Nonetheless, we believe that the present series, by illustrating how careful interpreters carry out their tasks, will encourage readers to be more reflective about the way they interpret the Bible.

Lloyd R. Bailey, Sr.
Duke Divinity School

Victor Paul Furnish
Perkins School of Theology
Southern Methodist University

CONTENTS

INTRODUCTION

Interpreting

You and I are interpreters. In fact, all of us are interpreters, and whether or not we refer to what we do as "interpreting," this activity is necessary for our handling the events and encounters of every day. Most of our interpreting is personal and subjective, our understanding and assimilating the sights and sounds, faces and words that enter our world and touch our lives. We are able to do this by reasoning, recalling prior experiences, and by drawing upon a lifetime of learning.

But occasionally events occur, words are read or heard, that we cannot interpret for ourselves. Lacking adequate resources for satisfactory understanding, we call upon others to serve as interpreters. Children look to parents as much for interpretations as for food and clothes. "What was that noise?" "Will Grandma have to stay dead very long?" "Do hamsters go to heaven?" and a thousand other questions are pleas for the parents to interpret the new and strange. Adults look to those with special qualifications as interpreters of the unfamiliar and disturbing. It may be a friend older and wiser, a lawyer, a minister, a physician, or a psychiatrist. It is

difficult to overstate the importance of this service we render
to each other, for without it, life itself could become
unbearable. A pain the doctor cannot interpret is twice as
sharp, and no tragedy is as heavy as one which none can
explain. Most interpreting, even that which we seem to do casually,
is not easy. And the difficulty is increased by two factors. One
factor is the importance of that which is to be interpreted. If it
is believed, for example, that a particular document will affect
the health or happiness or destiny, not only of the interpreter
of the document, but of all those who await an explanation,
then every word will be carefully weighed and pondered. The
other factor is the distance between the interpreter and that
which is to be interpreted. There is always some distance,
even between close friends or husband and wife, as evidenced
by the lines that sprinkle significant conversation: "If I
understand what you are saying"; "No, what I meant was"; "I
may have said that but what I intended. . . ." But there are
special kinds of distance difficult to negotiate. Think of the
distance of time; that which is to be interpreted may be fifty or
a hundred or a thousand years old. Then there are distances of
space, of language, of culture, of values and beliefs.

Consider an example of difficulty in interpreting because of
the presence of both factors, significance and distance.
Significance is present because that which is to be interpreted
is a document foundational and normative for the corporate
and private lives of millions: The Constitution of the United
States. The kind of distance involved is that of time; the
document is approximately two hundred years old. On
December 15, 1791, ten amendments to the Constitution
became effective. The second article of amendment states,
"The right of the people to keep and bear arms shall not be
infringed." What does that mean? The interpretation is

especially important and urgent now that the rate of crimes involving firearms is rising so sharply. One cannot necessarily "just take it for what it says." But who will give the interpretation? Shall each interpret for himself or herself? In the case of the Constitution, the final interpretation is made by the Supreme Court, but not easily or swiftly. Careful consideration is given to the original intent of the amendment, the conditions which prompted it, the conditions that now prevail, and the overall purpose of the Constitution to guarantee both security and freedom to all the citizens. How much heavier the task would be were the document centuries older, written in another language, and produced in and for another culture!

These comments are not intended to discourage those who would engage in interpreting, but rather to honor the task by recognizing its importance. Temptations to simplistic shortcuts should be resisted, for, while a document may sometimes yield its meaning immediately to sensitive intuition, most often it is only after study, questioning, and thought that understanding comes. But usually it does come.

Why do it? Why devote the time and effort to understand some ancient text and interpret its meaning for this time and place? The question is fair and appropriate. Perhaps it can be answered briefly in this way. Interpreting implies at least three things. First, interpreting implies that the document or text is very important to present readers. What was said or written to persons of another time and place is meaningful, perhaps authoritative, for persons here and now. Second, interpreting implies that the meaning of that document is not apparent at a first reading, but must be released by care and effort. And third, interpreting implies that previous understandings, however clear and firm, were not final and are not totally adequate for every time and place.[1] The circumstances and needs of new readers are ingredient to interpretation, and therefore make continuation of the process not only possible but necessary.

The assertion that interpretation is never final and complete may produce in some of us a degree of anxiety. If a message addressed to other people in another time and place is to be contemporized, is it not possible that in the translation something vital may be lost? Is there not too much at stake to open the doors to improvising and relativizing? This is a justifiable fear, but as long as this fear keeps sentinel watch over the interpretive process, the danger is sharply reduced. In addition, there are four conditions that offer assurance that interpretation may continue in healthy ways and not be paralyzed by the fear of gross misunderstandings that threaten to cut us off from traditions and sources of meaning. One condition, basic to all interpretation and without which it is impossible, is our common humanity. Regardless of distances of time and place and culture, human beings are more alike than different. A second assuring condition is the continuity with the past provided by the ongoing community which has preserved and valued the tradition being interpreted. Out of this continuity comes a third assurance: because the community has preserved and valued a recorded tradition, that document is very much a part of the present and not only of the past. In other words, much of the distance between the past and the present has already been negotiated by the very fact that the ancient tradition nourishes, instructs, and often determines present relationships, institutions, values, and even vocabulary. Again, recall the Bill of Rights amending the Constitution: there are

[1]For a fuller discussion of why interpretation is necessary, see Frank Kermode, *The Genesis of Secrecy* (Cambridge: Harvard University Press, 1979), pp. 143ff.

now two hundred years between that document and the present generation of Americans.

And finally, a fourth condition providing assurance of continuity is the presence in the community of that circle of specialists who bear the double responsibility of preserving the original tradition and of interpreting it for the present. It is a testimony to the central significance of the recorded tradition that this group exists in the community. Those who preserve and interpret may or may not have the formal structure and authority of a Supreme Court. They may or may not be recognized and received by the whole community. Their relationship to the community may be one of trust or suspicion. But through the vicissitudes of a people's history, the presence of this circle of specialists is protection against the loss or distortion of tradition either by the neglect of many or the private interpretations of a few. Not that these interpreters will do their work apart from the lively opinions of the community to whom they are finally responsible; of course not. Nor is it the case that the interpreters will always agree among themselves. However, debates among interpreters assure the whole community that the central tradition is alive and well, and its proper interpretation is not the unchallenged possession of a few.

Interpreting Scripture

You may have already sensed that while the paragraphs above pertain to interpreting the central tradition in any political or religious community, they are intended to bring us to thinking in particular about the interpretation of Scripture within the community of faith. In fact, everything said about the interpretation of the Constitution by and for the American people applies with increased force to the interpretation of Scripture by and for the church. Certainly the factors of significance and distance apply in larger measure and in greater complexity. Likewise, all the reasons why interpreting must be done are clear and strong as we turn to Scripture: the documents to be interpreted are as significant and authoritative to present readers as to the past; the meaning of the documents is not apparent to all readers; and changing needs and circumstances necessarily make interpretation an ongoing task. However, no less present are the conditions which assure that the messages of another time and place can be heard here and now. Centuries, continents, and cultures are bridged by a common humanity, and the unbroken continuity of the believing community negotiates distances that otherwise would be impossible chasms between the ancient texts and ourselves. The believing community has never ceased bringing the Bible forward into each generation, making it a part of present values, relationships, world views, and institutions. And wherever the church has gone, there has gone with it that circle of scholars within the circle of faith, preserving and providing the best possible copies of the ancient texts, good translations, and dictionaries, concordances, and commentaries. With the help of such resources, all members of the community of faith can participate in the interpretation of Scripture.

However, it would be a gross oversimplification to say that the analogy of interpreting the Constitution prepares one to move directly to interpreting Scripture. Before moving to the next step in our preparation, we must consider three topics: the relationship of the Bible to the church, the nature of the Bible, and basic procedural guidelines for interpretation. The reader will note several underlying assumptions in the discussion which follows. The articulation of basic assumptions serves honesty and clarity, and the benefits come not only to us but also to the communities in which we function as interpreters of Scripture.

The Bible and the church belong together. Martin Luther's principle of "Scripture alone," which became central in the Protestant Reformation, was never intended as an alternative to church, as though the decision were church *or* Scripture. On the contrary, Luther sought to correct a situation which could not be characterized as church *and* Scripture but as church *over* Scripture. Whenever the relationship between the community and the Book becomes unhealthy because either the church or the Bible has become dominant, errors and distortions follow. When the church has been dominant, voicing authority without coming under authority, judging without being judged, the institution and its dogmas have been marked by idolatry and superstition. When the Bible has been dominant without coming under the reflective judgment and interpretation of the community of faith, it, too, has been elevated in false reverence to idolatry and superstition. How, then, would one characterize a healthy relationship between the church and the Bible?

It is by no means a simple one. On the one hand, the Bible is the church's Book. The church embraced the Scriptures of the Jewish community as its own, adding to it the Christian writings that eventually comprised the New Testament. In the formation of the Christian Bible, the church functioned as writer, collector, and preserver. A very important criterion in the process of determining which writings were to be included in the canon was the practical judgment of a document's usefulness in the life and witness of the church. Once the canon was fixed, the church was diligent in protecting the Bible from corruption by additions, subtractions, or alterations. But the church was no less diligent in interpreting the Bible for new cultures, new circumstances, new generations. For example, Jesus gave his teaching on divorce in a context of Jewish law and custom; what did that teaching mean for believers in Rome or Alexandria? Or, what did the early confession "Jesus is

Messiah" mean to those not expecting a messiah? Or again, what
was to be the Christian attitude toward the state after Rome
shifted from quiet tolerance of Christianity to violent persecution? In order for the Bible to continue as a living voice, it had to
be interpreted. The church did that, bringing the messages of the
Bible forward into each new time, all the while seeking to
preserve continuity with the past and to be true to the tradition as
it was received. The church understood interpreting to be its
continuing responsibility since the Bible is the church's book.

On the other hand, the Bible is the church's Scripture. Simply
stated, this means the Bible is normative for shaping the life,
beliefs, and mission of the church. Therefore, the church sits
before the Bible to listen and to obey. Conduct, structures, and
programs come under the judgment of Scripture. Sometimes
even the church's interpretations of the Bible, however
sincerely and thoughtfully offered, may be called into question
and countered by the Bible itself. Interpreting necessarily
continues, but preceding and succeeding the entire process, the
text is always there to be reckoned with.

What, then, is the nature of this text, or rather, these texts
which constitute the Bible? For one approaching the Bible as an
interpreter, how can it be characterized? Descriptions of the
Bible can and do fill volumes, of course, but some interpreters
find themselves overwhelmed by the wealth of such resources.
Perhaps it would be helpful to fix in mind four terms to serve as
keys to understanding the nature of biblical materials.

The first term is *particularity*. The reader of the Bible is struck
by the frequent references to particular places, persons, events,
and dates. The interpreter will want to pursue these references
through biblical and extrabiblical sources in order to reconstruct the historical context. Unfortunately, for some references such historical recovery is not possible. But in either case,
what is most impressive is the character of biblical texts: they

arise out of, and address, concrete human conditions. Timeless truths spoken into the air to whom it may concern are rare in the Bible. As we shall discuss shortly, interpretive methods and procedures will need to take this particularity into account.

The second term is *integrity*. Here this word is used to characterize, not the Bible as a whole, but the particular perspectives of the individual books and writers within it. Of course the Bible as a single book has integrity; that is, a unity in its subject matter, but it is also a collection of many books, each of which has its own integrity. This latter fact is sometimes forgotten when an interpreter too hastily summarizes "what the Bible says." Books lying side by side in the Bible may be very distant from each other in time, circumstance, and geographical setting. Even in the New Testament, which was written over a relatively brief period of time, the turn of one page can transport the reader from one continent to another, from one generation to another, and from one church to another church that has very different needs and problems. The eye moves swiftly and easily from Romans to First Corinthians, but the interpreter who respects the integrity of a writing will move carefully and thoughtfully from Rome to Corinth. It is especially important to remember this when dealing with two or more writings that treat the same subject matter, as do Paul's letters and the latter part of Acts, or more conspicuously, the four Gospels. To be sure, one must consider the way these documents bear upon each other, but allowing their messages to bleed into each other and blend as though written by a single author is hardly responsible interpretation.

The third term is *continuity*. The literature of the Bible spans hundreds of years, but across those centuries the stories move forward without loss of contact with the past. At times this continuity is evidenced by the repetition of the traditions more or less exactly as received (note, e.g., 1 Cor 11:23ff. and

15:3ff.). But more commonly the continuity was preserved by fresh interpretations of the past appropriate to the new circumstances of the believing community. Perhaps the Gettysburg Address can serve as a helpful analogy. In that speech President Lincoln took the rhetoric of freedom and equality forged in the struggle with England four score and seven years earlier and gave it a new interpretation in the context of a raging civil war. In similar fashion, an anonymous writer (or writers) produced Deuteronomy, which is not a repetition of Exodus but an interpretation of what Moses *is saying* to seventh-century Israel in the days of King Josiah. Likewise, Jewish messianic hopes were not only revived, but reviewed and interpreted with the appearance of John and Jesus. The confession "Jesus is Messiah" was translated by Paul in order to give it meaning for his gentile churches. Jesus' teaching on divorce, framed for a Jewish audience, had to be interpreted anew to answer questions in a church in Corinth, Greece (1 Cor 7:10-16). Words implying an imminent return of Christ (Mark 9:1; Matt 10:23) had to be understood in a new way after much time passed and cynical doubts were eroding Christian hope (2 Pet 3:3-11). Thus do the texts both preserve and modify the ongoing tradition. As in all interpretation, however, the movement was not solely from past to present; the present was also interpreted in light of the past. Let the modern interpreter be assured, therefore, that he or she is not engaged in a foreign and strange intrusion into the texts but rather is continuing the process to which the Scriptures themselves bear witness and of which the Scriptures themselves are the fruit.

The fourth and final term by which we are seeking to focus upon the nature of the Bible is *diversity* of literature. The range of literary forms is surprisingly broad, representative of the kinds of literature available in the general culture which were found useful. The casual reader of the Bible cannot fail to recognize many of these forms: genealogies, legal codes, prayers, oracles, court records, biographies, poems, creeds, parables, public addresses, correspondence, apocalypses, visions, miracle stories, doxologies. The more careful reader will likely reflect upon the various settings in which these forms were employed: worship, instruction of the young, funerals, coronations, debate with other religions, festivals, community crises, evangelism. The interpreter of Scripture will go even farther, analyzing the forms of the texts, reconstructing where possible the life settings in which the texts functioned, and determining in what new life settings these materials may be recontexted appropriately and meaningfully. In addition, the interpreter will be alert to what forms *do* as well as what they *say*. A poem *does* something, a parable *does* something, in addition to conveying a message. The wide variety of forms of literature in the Bible provides a multitude of rich experiences for the person spending time in the texts.

Having considered briefly the relationship between the Bible and the church, and the nature of the Bible, there remains at this stage of our discussion the third and final topic—some procedural guidelines for interpreting scripture. As we move to a brief sketch of such guidelines, perhaps we should remind ourselves that interpretation has its entire rationale in the two subjects discussed above: the relationship of the Bible and the church provides the mandate and the nature of the Bible provides the method. Mandate, not simply permission, is the proper word here, for mandate best expresses the responsibility implicit in the double truth that the Bible is the church's book and that it is the church's Scripture. As to method, it will be evident that the procedures suggested here arise directly from the nature of the Bible as characterized above. As with all subject matter procedures for understanding should be congenial to that which is to be understood. On this principle the following Procedural Guidelines for interpretation are offered.

1. Directly engage the text to be interpreted, reading it several times, at least once aloud. Release all faculties of thought, feeling, and imagination to respond immediately, without the restraint of what one *should* think and feel. Several important things happen at this first step: honest opening of the self and the text to each other, the beginning of ownership of the lesson or sermon to come later (commentaries introduced too soon allow experts to take over the conversation), and identification with listeners who will have similar thoughts and feelings when the text is shared publicly. This engagement with the text will then move from the spontaneous to the deliberate as a careful analysis of the passage is made. The interpreter will thus be prepared to move later to commentaries and dictionaries with a sense of being a colleague of the specialists rather than being overwhelmed by them.

2. Set the text in its historical context, reconstructing the particularities of time, place, and circumstance. Dictionaries, atlases, introductions, and commentaries will be most useful here. The important thing is not to allow an impatience for immediacy and relevance to collapse the distance between past and present. This very distance and strangeness can stir the imagination.

To say the text is historically conditioned is to say it bears witness that the gospel had to encounter and make its way in a world of demons, superstition, subordination of women, political and economic oppression, primitive world views, and plurality of religions. The gospel at times affirmed, at times modified, and at times opposed prevailing structures of value and life patterns. To peel away all the concrete particularities of the text in order to seek a timeless truth behind "all that primitive stuff" is to miss the struggle of the gospel, sometimes winning, sometimes losing, in real human situations. Similarly, we are in a world quite foreign to that of the Bible, a world in which the gospel has to make its way amid structures of prejudice, militarism, business and industrial complexes, economic determinism, pluralism, mobility of population, short-term relationships, and changing values. We do not run to the Bible to hide from the pressures and problems of our technocratic society. Rather we seek to understand how the gospel comes to terms with, affirms, opposes, and seeks to transform specific situations in a given time and place. Of course, the distance between then and now will sometimes appear immense. However, if historical reconstruction is done with honesty and imagination, analogies and points of identification between past and present will emerge and dialogue with the text will open up. One need not force the text to be "meaningful" by punctuating interpretation with hortatory remarks, such as, "How like the Pharisees we are today!"

3. Set the text in its literary context, seeking to discern the intention of the writer. A text may not mean only what a writer intended, but it certainly means at least that much. This concern for intent respects the integrity of each book and guards against one's accumulating all the references the Bible offers on the subject at hand and treating them as though written by one person to one situation. One can be seduced by a concordance. In fact, one cannot assume that the three readings from the lectionary for a given Sunday can be easily blended into one statement.

Some interpreters will probably feel too constrained by this emphasis upon intention, and rightly so, if it is taken as the sole guide to the meaning of a text. To call these texts Scripture is to say that in a sense they have a life of their own, their authority residing in part in their ability to speak a clear word to a variety of situations beyond the author's own context or intention. But to go to the extreme of disregarding intention, of granting such autonomy to the texts that, as with some approaches to art, meaning lies entirely in the eye of the beholder, is to turn interpretation into ink-blot tests. Too large a door is opened to privatism and subjectivism. Interpreters are members of a community that receives and passes along the tradition, and concern for intent not only respects that fact, but acts as a safeguard against radical discontinuity. Just as Beethoven's music could be so employed as to cease to be *Beethoven's* music, so Mark's Gospel, for example, could cease to be *Mark's* Gospel.

4. Determine if the text being interpreted had a history prior to its appearance in its present location. Since some of the Old Testament is recontexted and reinterpreted in the Old Testament, some of the Old in the New, and some of the New in the New, tracing this process can be most helpful both in understanding how the community made use of its traditions and in providing some general guidelines for further interpretation. For example, in 1 Cor 10:1 ff., Paul interprets an interpretation of the Exodus in order to warn the morally careless Christians in Corinth. Or, as we shall observe shortly, Matthew and Luke interpreted Mark's interpretation of materials about Jesus. The act of bringing the text into the present is most responsible if it exhibits concern for continuity.

5. Seek to keep the form of the text intact throughout the interpretive process. From start to finish form functions in many ways. Form aids in locating natural breaking points for isolating a unit as one asks where the parable, exorcism, pronouncement, healing, or prayer begins and ends. Changes within the form of a text as well as comments surrounding it make possible the tracing of the history of that text (if it has a history) through various interpretations. Form opens the door

to the life of the early church and grants access not only to what those believers were saying but to what they were doing: singing, confessing, instructing, debating, evangelizing. And as far as possible, the final interpretation in a lesson or sermon should seek to maintain the form of the text. Of course, the interpretation of a prayer does not have to be prayed nor does that of a psalm have to be sung. However, it is a worthy goal to have the lesson or sermon participate in what the text does as well as what it says. Too often the final product is a distillation of ideas and meanings gleaned from the text with the original form discarded in the process. In some cases the loss is enormous. If in the process of interpreting, a parable ceases to be a parable and becomes a proposition; if a beatitude ceases to be a blessing and becomes an exhortation, not only form but experience and meaning have been altered. Communication of interpretation is itself interpretation.

6. Understand the present situation in which the text is being heard. This is not, of course, one single step in the process to be done between steps five and seven. The present of the interpreter and of the community was doubtless involved as early as the choosing of the text to be shared. Certainly one has to acknowledge that present needs and preconceptions have influenced all along what has been seen and heard in the text. But the point here is that the present no less than the past needs careful interpretation. One cannot simply assume that living in a world means understanding it. There are formal avenues to be taken: reading and structured opportunities for learning. There are also informal avenues: active participation in the life of the community and empathetic sharing in the experiences of others. Only in this way can the interpreter overcome the temptation to identify with Paul and assume the listeners are Corinthians or Galatians, or identify with Jesus and assume the listeners are Pharisees or confused disciples. When the interpreter takes his or

her place among those who hear rather than those who dispense the Scriptures, the process acquires that quality most essential in interpreting a text: appropriateness.

7. Finally, let the interpreter be content to bring the text to bear on the here and now and drop any ambition to divine a truth that is for all persons and for all ages. It is tempting to entertain the notion that one's study has discerned the single sense of the text and that final closure is now possible. One may hope that much of what one does in analyzing a text will stand the test of time, but to call these texts Scripture is to say they are continually to be heard anew. The Word of God is never in the past tense.

Some readers may have noticed the absence of statements about the role of the Holy Spirit in the interpretation of Scripture. This is not an omission due to doubt as to the presence of the Spirit in the writing, selecting, and continuing appropriation of Scripture by the church. It is rather due to the firm conviction that the Holy Spirit cannot be made a *calculated* factor in any of our work. We may hope the Spirit can use us and our interpretations, but we are not to *use* the Spirit.

Interpreting the Gospels

Interpreting selected texts from the four Gospels is the central concern of this volume. Before we move to that task, however, three matters need brief attention: the nature of a Gospel, special interpretive problems presented by a Gospel, and criteria for selecting the texts to be interpreted.

First, what is a "Gospel?" The term as used to designate a kind of literature probably originated when the first line of Mark was abbreviated as if it had been intended as the title for that book: "The beginning of the gospel of Jesus Christ, the Son of God." If any of the forms of literature in the New Testament is original with the Christian community, it is the Gospel. This is not to say that all the materials in the canonical Gospels are without literary parallel in the Jewish, Greek, or Roman culture. "Biographies" of men of ancient times regarded as divine or closely related to the divine by reason of moral excellence or wisdom or miraculous power often consisted of collections of sayings, or miracles, or revelations. We recognize such literary forms in New Testament Gospels. In fact, some of the sources available to the Gospel writers may have been materials about Jesus formulated according to the patterns of just such pagan biographies.[2] Some scholars believe that the literary patterns of pagan biographies are most clearly imitated in Christian literature in what we call Apocryphal Gospels, narratives about Jesus not accepted in the New Testament which consist almost totally of saying, miracles, or revelations.

The canonical Gospels are distinguished by their inclusion of a variety of types of material about Jesus, as well as by the fact that these materials are interpreted under the control of one governing theme: Jesus of Nazareth is the crucified and risen Lord. In other words, the gospel of the early church (Paul gives us its classic formulation as the tradition received and passed on in 1 Cor 15:1-5) was the norm at work in the selection and interpretation of stories about Jesus' words and deeds, so that the canonical Gospels are narrative elaborations of the gospel. Whatever may have been the sources, written and oral, and whatever may have been the uses of those sources in the circles where they arose (sayings of the Master Teacher, revelations of the Eternal Logos, miracles of the Divine Man), in the canonical Gospels they are woven into a narrative interpreting Jesus in the light of the cross and resurrection.

Given this overall factor of control over the sources available to the Gospel writers, other considerations also entered into the

[2]Charles Talbert, *What Is a Gospel?* (Philadephia: Fortress Press, 1977).

selection and interpretation of those sources. Since the Gospels were written not just "to whom it may concern" but to particular Christian communities, then one would expect the needs of those communities to be addressed. The churches needed to be equipped for the usual tasks of evangelizing, teaching new converts, and worshiping. But there were other needs related to the facing of problems within and without: persecution, tension with the Jewish community, political fervor and zealotism, intense focus upon the return of Christ or a collapse of all expectation of his return, defection to false prophets, erosion of moral and ethical earnestness under the influence of escapist spiritualism, or rejection of the Jesus of the cross in favor of the Christ from heaven. As would any responsible preacher or pastor, the Gospel writers sought not only to *preserve* the gospel under such circumstances but to *interpret* it so as to address the issues vital to the life and faith of the church. To the extent that they told the stories of Jesus so as to preserve and proclaim the gospel, we may expect them to be similar; to the extent that they had to address that gospel to a variety of issues facing the particular churches to whom they wrote, we may expect them to be different from each other.

How will those differences be manifest to the reader of the Gospels? By the writers' selection of stories available from all that Jesus said and did; by the arrangement of the materials so that by the location of an event or a saying the desired meaning is conveyed; by editorial expansion or abbreviation of the received material; or by comments introducing or concluding the account of an act or a teaching of Jesus.

Perhaps an analogy will bring the discussion closer to our own experience. Suppose your church is going to honor one of its faithful leaders upon retirement. This is to be done in the form of a program patterned after the once-popular television show, *This Is Your Life*. Through weeks of correspondence, interviews, and phone calls, about thirty stories from the private and public life of the honoree have been gathered and are to be woven into a narrative to be read for the occasion. How are the stories to be arranged? Chronologically, from birth to the present? Perhaps beginning with the present and then moving backward? Or perhaps clustered around key topics, such as home life, education, marriage, vocation, religious activity? Or it may be more appropriate to arrange the stories in relation to critical moments in the honoree's life. Or why not let all the selections be controlled by the one major impact this person has made upon the community? Quite possibly the stories might be arranged so as to correct some misunderstandings about this person. For example, stories of courageous leadership could be followed by selections that revealed qualities of tender reticence, or accounts of discipline and austerity might be joined immediately and without comment to vignettes reflecting childlike playfulness. The stories are all there; intention will weave them into a narrative.

A writer has in the sources available the sayings and the events for a narrative about Jesus Christ. A church has needs to be addressed. The intersection of the two is called a Gospel, a literary work of immense courage and freedom. On what ground could anyone be so bold and free with the stories about Jesus of Nazareth? One could do so on the conviction that this Jesus is the living Lord of the church, still speaking the appropriate and authoritative word in every new circumstance, yet a word which is in no way discontinuous with the life and activity of Jesus of Nazareth.

What, then, are the special problems presented to the interpreter by such literature? Procedurally it will probably be best to deal with particular problems as they arise out of the texts being interpreted. However, most of those specific problems will be related to one of two overarching facts: we have four different Gospels concerning the one person Jesus Christ, and we have in each Gospel evidence of layers of interpretations of Jesus' words and deeds.

The existence of four Gospels and the occurrences in them of two or three or even four narrations of any one event has from early times been a cause of perplexity in the church. For those who ask the texts only the historical question, What really happened? this has been especially true. From the second century effort of Tatian to create one Gospel out of four until the present, various harmonies of the Gospels have abounded. Unfortunately, these have nourished the tendency of some in the church to extract from the Gospels a life of Jesus captured in topics: birth, baptism, healing the blind, cleansing the temple, etc. Thinking topically rather than textually blurs distinctions that otherwise are both clear and significant, as, for example, between Matthew and Mark on the baptism of Jesus, or between Mark and John on cleansing the temple or healing the blind. These distinctions: arrangement of the stories, perspective in narration, and brief commentary within and surrounding a unit of material, reveal the Gospel writer's intent in preserving and interpreting the tradition about Jesus. These distinctions are therefore important to the interpreter who respects the integrity of each Gospel and the intention of each writer. In other words, not a topic, but the text is the matter to be interpreted.

As to layers of interpretation within the Gospels, it is generally accepted that the canonical Gospels preserve materials from the career of Jesus, circulated and used in the early church, and interpreted by the writers to meet the needs of those addressed. Careful attention to the text will often enable a reader to discern these different stages in the history of the tradition. However, it is not uncommon to hear a teacher or preacher share the Gospel texts as though all the content were from the level of Jesus' own words and deeds. The interpreter will want to be more careful. If a text contains an earlier tradition, whether it be an Old Testament quotation or a saying or act of Jesus, that fact will be noted and a decision made as to which level of the tradition is to be interpreted for classroom or pulpit. For example, if one can distinguish in Luke 16:1ff. between Jesus' parable and Luke's interpretation of it, then one needs to decide from which level the lesson or sermon will proceed. One does not engage in such an exercise, however, on the assumption that "earlier" is more authoritative than "later," or vice versa.

Having considered what a Gospel is and reflected on certain interpretive problems peculiar to that literature, we come to the third and final matter: the criteria for selecting texts to be interpreted.

Only a limited number of texts can be dealt with here, but these have been selected carefully in order to illustrate what is involved in interpreting the Gospels. The following concerns have guided the selection process: (1) all four Gospels should receive basically the same amount of attention, and any one Gospel should not be favored; (b) a text representative of each Gospel's basic perspective should be included; (c) the texts should provide opportunity for working with a variety of literary genres; (d) the selections should be adequately representative of gospel materials so that efforts expended on these examples will have carry-over value in one's work on similar texts; (e) the texts should vary in length; (f) at least some of the selections should be such as are common (with variation) to two or more of the Gospels, so as to add the comparative dimension to the process of interpretation; (g) the selections should be judged to have points of clear intersection with the church today. (We must beware here lest texts be "used" and pressed into service. It is my judgment that the content of the texts themselves will forestall such use.) In addition it will be noted that the texts selected for interpretation are of varying degrees of difficulty for both thought and faith.

To satisfy all seven concerns the number of texts chosen grew beyond early projections. The price paid for more selections was, of course, brevity of discussion. But if not too severely trimmed, the pruned branch bears more fruit.

THE GOSPEL OF MARK

The writing of the Gospel of Mark was a landmark event in the literary activity of the Christian community. It was not the first literature of the church. At least a generation earlier Paul had written letters to the churches, and even those contained quoted materials, indicating Paul had literary predecessors. A careful reading of Mark reveals that he, too, had sources, perhaps written as well as oral. But most scholars believe that Mark was the first to produce a Gospel as such. His work opened the door to a flood of others. Luke says that many had taken up the task of recording what Jesus said and did (Luke 1:1-4). We now possess or know of several dozen Gospels, and at least two, Matthew and Luke, are heavily indebted to Mark for both form and content.

Precisely what prompted the writing of Mark is not clear. One may presume that there was a concern to preserve the stories that otherwise might be lost through the fading of memory and the deaths of witnesses. But what other factors were at work? In Mark, the ministry of Jesus is in Galilee, except for the one fateful journey to Jerusalem. Is this Gospel, then, an expression of Galilean Christianity to counter the rise of Jerusalem to prominence and authority? Mark moves the story of Jesus to the cross with the single-mindedness of a Good Friday sermon. Has persecution arisen so as to call the church again to cross-bearing? Or perhaps the Easter faith has been presented to Mark's church in a way that has distorted, if not erased, the real costs of discipleship. Has the fall of Jerusalem stirred some prophets to announce the end time, against which proclamation Mark was compelled to write "the end is not yet" (13:7)? Some are convinced Mark entered his Gospel into the christological debate: Jesus the crucified Lord or Jesus the miracle worker from heaven? Still others interpret the portrayal of the Twelve as blind, afraid, confused, and unbelieving as a Markan vendetta against the apostles. Theories abound, thanks to the germinal brevity and the revealing/concealing language of this Gospel.

But regardless of anyone's conclusions as to why, when, where, and by whom it was written, the Gospel of Mark (along with the three canonical Gospels that followed) has significance beyond estimation for any attempts to understand Christianity. Mark shows us that Jesus of Nazareth is the central figure to be dealt with. Mark shows us that the Christian faith cannot be evaporated into visions or ecstatic insights, and that the Gospel cannot be captured in the subjectivity of a believer's experience. Mark also shows us that the Christian proclamation involves not only the confrontation of a hearer by the crucified and risen Lord, but also a narrative recital of what Jesus said and did. Because of Mark, at least one definition of discipleship is following in the way of Jesus.

This is not to say that the Gospel of Mark is a presentation of "just the facts." There was a time when Mark's brevity, abrupt transitions, and general literary awkwardness were regarded as evidence in the case for this being a bare historical account. This view became widespread at a time when many recognized in

Matthew, Luke, and John a great deal of interpretation of the career of Jesus, but at the same time sought basic unadorned, uninterpreted information about Jesus as a sure foundation for belief. But that time has passed; this Gospel now joins the others as a major theological work. Mark has something he wants to say to the church, and he does it by the selection of certain units of material, by a thoughtful, and often dramatic, arrangement of those units, and by the cementing of the various stories with brief introductions and conclusions, thus forming a continuous narrative about Jesus. When interpreting Mark, that fact should take precedence over one's desire to reconstruct the chronology, itinerary, and specific events of Jesus' ministry. If anyone insists upon a chronology, Mark offers only a fast-paced ministry apparently encompassing less than one year. If geography is important, the scenes of Jesus' work are in and around Galilee until that fateful trip to Jerusalem. If an outline to the narrative is needed, Mark is even more hesitant to yield that. Some scholars have discerned in the confession of Peter and the first prediction of the passion (8:27-33) a watershed between a popular ministry amid the crowds in Galilee and a period of preparing his disciples as they move toward Jerusalem.

However, the reader should stake very little upon such tentative and scantily supported reconstructions. It is far more fruitful to search afresh for Mark's message to his readers. In the pursuit of that, one can expect discoveries about Jesus and the early Christian community. To aid this exploration of Mark (and the other Gospels as well) review the suggested procedural guidelines and the brief description of what a Gospel is. In order to develop the habit of working directly with the text itself, perhaps three exercises need to be underscored:

1) Read the whole of Mark (it should take about two hours), jotting notes of immediate impressions and questions.

2) When moving to a particular unit to be interpreted, repeat

the above and then prepare a careful sketch or outline of the
passage. Especially note introductory and concluding comments; the setting of the event or saying; location of the unit in
relation to other units (arranging materials is a way of providing
commentary without commenting); recurring phrases or
themes; and any disjunctures within the passage itself.

3) Note any analogies or points of identification between
one's present situation and the events, characterizations, or
ideas in the text. These may be modified, clarified, or even
rejected once work in Bible dictionaries and commentaries is
done. However, other concordances may emerge. In either
case, this process of clarification and correction of apparent
analogies and similarities is vital to honest interpretation.

The interpretations of selected passages from Mark and the
other Gospels which constitute the remainder of this book
assume that this preliminary work has been done. The
unprepared are not allowed beyond this point!

Mark 1:21-28
An Exorcism in Capernaum

It is evident that 1:21-28 is to be treated as one unit. It opens
with a new time, place, and activity, quite distinct from the
preceding verses; a concluding summary is offered in v 28; there
is noticeable symmetry with vv 27-28 returning to the content of
vv 21-22; the following verse introduces a new place and
activity. If there appears to be any lack of unity in the
paragraph, it is due to the noticeable fact that the opening and
closing statements focus upon Jesus' authoritative teaching and
its effect on the crowds, while the activity of Jesus at the center
of the passages is an exorcism. A crowd is amazed at Jesus'
teaching with authority. They see him exorcise a demon. As a
result, apparently, of watching an exorcism, they are amazed at
his *teaching*. What is the connection between his teaching and

exorcism? The unexpected response demands our return for a more careful look.

• Here the structure of the passage itself is being examined.

But first, let us see this paragraph in the larger context.

• The purpose here will be to look for clues concerning the writer's use of the story and his reasons for placing it just here in the overall narrative. See Procedural Guideline 3, p. 21.

This is the second in a series of six brief episodes with which Mark describes the beginning of Jesus' ministry (1:16-39). By way of introduction Mark has briefly but dramatically opened with the wilderness scene so familiar in Israel's history and literature. John, the wilderness prophet, is preaching, baptizing, and announcing the approach of the Kingdom. Jesus comes from Nazareth and is baptized, at which time he experiences that special relation to God which Mark thinks of as "sonship," and beholds the signs of the launching of the new age. The Spirit drives Jesus into the wilderness for forty days where he is tempted by Satan. The language is brief but powerful and suggestive of intense conflict: tempted-Satan-wild beasts-angels. The next two verses (14-15) provide transition (John is arrested, Jesus comes to Galilee) and introduce Jesus' ministry (preaching the gospel, announcing the arrival of the Kingdom, calling for repentance and faith). Verses 16-39 become interior to that ministry and offer snapshots of what it involved: call of followers, teaching, exorcism, healing, and traveling throughout Galilee. As a result Jesus was immensely popular.

Beginning at verse 21, the stories are generally held together by the image of a sabbath-day's activity: in the synagogues, later to a private home, crowds come at sunset, early morning prayer, and departure on a Galilean itinerary. By means of this "a day in the life of Jesus" arrangement, Mark is providing the reader, at the very outset of his Gospel, a digest of the entire ministry. The verses immediately before us have a special prominence within this digest: they contain the account of Jesus' first miracle, enclosed in more Markan commentary than accompanies any of the other stories.

In Mark's narrative, the first miracle of Jesus was an exorcism (1:23-26). Performing an exorcism did not put Jesus in a class by himself; the literature of the period relates exorcisms by Jewish and Gentile leaders. The New Testament is well aware of this (Matt 12:27; Luke 11:19). Nor does the manner in which Mark tells it depart noticeably from the rather fixed pattern for exorcism stories: (1) the demon recognizes the exorcist and puts up a struggle; (2) the exorcist threatens and commands; (3) the demon comes out with loud and violent demonstrations; (4) the spectators are amazed.[3] It is striking that of all the varieties of acts performed in Jesus' ministry, an exorcism would be offered as a paradigm of what he was doing.

But the whole of Mark's Gospel reveals how deliberately this choice was made. As we know, in that culture demons were regarded as crippling and evil forces attacking body, mind, and spirit. They were many, they were organized under the power of Satan, they inhabited the air above, the earth, and the abyss. Their intent was to thwart, to sabotage the will of God that was at work for life and good. According to Mark, Jesus as the bringer of the good news of the Kingdom threw himself into battle against the forces of evil. That such struggles would occur is intimated in the account of the temptation. The battle is joined, with Jesus, the healer, attacking and being attacked. He is the strong one who enters Satan's house, binds him, and

---

[3]See the articles on "Exorcism" in *The Interpreter's Dictionary of the Bible* (Nashville: Abingdon, 1962, 1976), vols. 2 and 5.

plunders his goods (3:27). Mark's Jesus is not the pensive loner, walking in the garden with lowered eyes and folded hands. He counters the power of the enemy, whether that enemy surfaces in the lives of the crippled and deranged, among religious leaders who stand against him (2:1–3:6), within his own circle of friends (8:33), or even in the forces of nature that would destroy life (4:37-39).

But perhaps even more striking than his choice of an exorcism as an illustration of Jesus' ministry is Mark's interpretation of exorcism by prefacing the story with vv 21-22 and closing it with vv 27-28. It is clear from Mark's characteristic "and immediately" that he is introducing at v 21 and at v 23 (again at v 29) units that are distinct and may have been separate in his sources. Matthew's use of v 22 at the close of the Sermon on the Mount is further indication that this statement probably existed apart from the setting Mark provides in v 21 and the exorcism story which follows. Likewise, Mark resumes the accent on Jesus' teaching following the exorcism. The amazed spectators said, "What is this? A new teaching?" Immediately our curiosity is aroused: why would the response to an exorcism be the question of whether Jesus is offering a new *teaching*? That disjuncture may provide the key to Mark's point here.

Consider this possibility: Mark has received this story of Jesus' work as exorcist. He could have omitted it from his account (Matthew did), since he most likely had in his sources many other things Jesus said and did. But Mark preserved it, not simply because of a concern to describe all phases of Jesus' public ministry, but because it is totally in accord with Mark's understanding of Jesus as the strong opponent of the forces of evil that cripple human life. However, Mark does not want the picture of Jesus the exorcist, the miracle worker, to stand alone, uninterpreted. Why? Several possibilities come to mind. Exorcism alone does not generate faith in Jesus as Son of God.

In fact, an exorcism is capable of creating, not only confusion and misunderstanding, but even the interpretation that the miracle is not of God. Mark says on one occasion that Jesus' friends tried to seize him, thinking he was beside himself, and that scribes from Jerusalem said he was possessed by Beelzebub (3:19b-22). In our world, the response to a miracle claim is, "Did it really happen?" but in that world the question was, "Who did it, God or Satan?"

Another possible reason for Marks's interpreting Jesus' power to exorcise demons by placing this story in a context of teaching was to subdue an aspect of Jesus' ministry that was being enlarged or overemphasized in the church. Mark records, not only Jesus' activity as miracle worker, but also those occasions on which the miraculous is absent (he *could not* do any mighty work, 6:5), or accomplished with difficulty (healing a blind man with a second effort, 8:22-26), or sharply minimized (tell no one, 1:43-44, 5:43 *et al.*). If Mark's church included those who put a high premium on the divine power of the Son of God and therefore made miracles central in the ministry of the church (we know such persons were in other churches, Matt 7:21-23; 2 Cor 10–13), then we can understand Mark's corrective here. We will discuss later, at 8:27-33, the secrecy motif in Mark, but it is appropriate to note here that for Mark an *informed* confession of faith in Jesus Christ did not come in the midst of miracles, but had to wait upon the central events of crucifixion and resurrection (9:9).

A third and not unrelated explanation for Mark's interpreting an exorcism in terms of Jesus' teaching ministry is that the primary image of Jesus he wishes to convey is that of teacher. Any other image, such as miracle worker, is not to compete with that of teacher, but rather to be seen as one expression of the overarching description of Jesus as teaching with authority and power. This characteristic of Mark's narrative can be easily missed simply because Mark gives us so little of the content of what Jesus taught. When one thinks of teaching one thinks of subject matter, and in that respect Matthew and Luke take precedence over Mark. Perhaps Mark assumed his readers already knew the content of the teaching. Some students of Mark have theorized that the scarcity of actual teachings is a reaction or corrective to the circulation of so-called Gospels that consisted solely of sayings, presumably similar to the Gnostic *Gospel of Thomas*. If such Gospels actually existed, and if they were used by "heretical" groups, then Mark's focus on authoritative acts as teaching would be a reasonable corrective. Of course, there may have been some other reason for including so little of the content of Jesus' teaching. Even so, Mark, more than Matthew or Luke, calls Jesus "Teacher," a fact partially obscured by the translation "Master" in some places where the word in Greek is clearly "Teacher." More importantly, "Teacher" is Mark's term for Jesus in miracle situations: casting out a demon (1:21-28), stilling the storm (4:35), raising Jairus' daughter (5:35), responding compassionately to hungry crowds (6:34), healing an epileptic boy (9:17), cursing a fig tree (11:21), and others. For Mark, the important fact about Jesus' teaching was not the lesson that was taught, although content is not totally absent (e.g., the parables of chap. 4), but the power and authority of his word. He commanded and his word was power: demons fled, storms ceased, the dead were raised, the sick were healed, the opponents were silenced, the Twelve were in awe, and the crowds were astonished.

Mark wants the church he addresses to know that the word of Jesus Christ is the word of power. This is not to satisfy historical interest about Jesus as a teacher, but to confirm, to encourage, to correct, to challenge the church. That word of Christ, he says, continues in the church. "Whoever loses his life for my sake *and the gospel's* will save it" (8:35). "For whoever is

ashamed of me and *of my words* in this adulterous and sinful
generation . . ." (8:38). As we shall see in 16:1-8, Mark's Jesus,
following the resurrection, "is not here." There are no
resurrection appearances, there is no promise to be with them
always. He will, he says, go before them into Galilee. In the
meantime, what does the church do? Live on memories of the
ministry of Jesus? No; there is the Gospel, there is his word of
power.

• The interpreter will have to make a decision, based upon a
reading of the present situation, about the point of intersection
between the text and the believing community. On the one hand,
Mark's use of the tradition can be followed: enclose the miracle in
an emphasis upon Jesus's teaching ministry. Such would be
appropriate for listeners who extract miracles from context,
translate Christianity as a flow of divine favors, think of faith as
the way to health, prosperity, and a perennial smile, and define
church as a soul spa. Radio and TV sell this religion daily. To such
a view Mark's word is still on target: Jesus' power to effect change
is conveyed in his teaching. Our entire culture suffers from a
failure to see the role of the teacher and the power of teaching.
Likewise the church's giving little planning to teaching, less
preparation, and even less time and money has hardly continued
Jesus' ministry. Where does the church stir the crowds to say,
"What is this? A new teaching!"

On the other hand, the interpreter may decide the better course
would be to deal with the text at the level of the tradition Mark
received: Jesus performs an exorcism. To a church that sums up its
life in terms of "accepting and being accepted" this exorcism story
is strong reminder that Jesus threw himself into battle against the
forces that cripple, distort, and destroy human life. To follow
Jesus is to oppose evil, personal and impersonal. A tranquilized
society seeks to avoid a hassle at any cost, but the church of Jesus
Christ does not. The interpreter in his or her own context should
have no major problem moving from first-century demons to
twentieth-century forms of assault, no less demonic, upon body,

mind, and spirit. One will also notice that Jesus' conflict with evil occurred in a synagogue, a humbling reminder that even the structures of religion may house forces that oppose the Gospel.

Mark 2:1-12
Healing and Forgiveness

Few texts in Mark stir the number and variety of questions aroused by the passage before us.

● Let the questions arise as they will, without worrying about whether they are the "proper" questions. See Procedural Guideline 1, p. 20.

Was Jesus at home in Capernaum or just *in a house?* Did the paralytic have no faith, and did he become a beneficiary of Jesus' power simply because his friends had faith? Are we to understand from the story that sin and disease are related? If so, why did not forgiveness heal the disease? Why did there also have to be a word of healing? If Jesus blasphemed, an act punishable by death, why was no action taken against him here? If blasphemy is committed here, why did not that act, rather than the healing, capture the crowd, filling them with amazement and wonder? How does healing a cripple show that Christ has power to forgive sins? Questions keep coming, very likely more than we will be able to handle, but this passage will provide occasion for a number of valuable exercises in interpreting Gospel materials. We will see how and perhaps why stories about Jesus were gathered into discernible collections, our text being a part of one such collection; we can see how Mark as an interpreter uses an unusual literary device to put an issue into focus sharply and persuasively; and we will hear in the text one of the most important and at the same time most controversial claims of the Christian community, a claim grounded in the activity of Jesus himself.

● First, however, it is important to be sure the passage is a unit with a clearly defined beginning and ending. Failure to attend to this early step in interpretation can create confusion, and sometimes distortion, of a text. Once the unit of material is seen in its own integrity, then, of course, it is placed again into the narrative.

Clearly 2:1 begins a unit distinct from the preceding account. In typical fashion, Mark introduces the story with a shift in Jesus' itinerary, the naming of the location, and a vague reference to time ("after some days"). The idiom translated "at home" implies that Jesus now resides in Capernaum. Likewise, Mark provides a typical conclusion that all who saw were amazed. Verse 13, by shifting the scene, obviously begins a new unit. The only problem concerning the unity of 2:1-12 lies in its center where a story of forgiving sin divides in half a story of healing a cripple.

From a careful reading of the whole Gospel, it is clear that 2:1 introduces, not only the story of 2:1-12, but a series of stories ending at 3:6. There are five of these stories bound together by one theme: conflict with religious leaders. The issues are clear: forgiving sins, eating with sinners, fasting, observing the Sabbath. Before continuing his narrative, Mark rounds off this section by describing a collaboration in plotting Jesus' death. This sentence concludes the entire section and not just 3:1-5. Otherwise, the interpreter faces the awkward problem of explaining why a death scheme developed after an argument over Sabbath breaking when there was none after the charge of blasphemy earlier. Blasphemy was the gravest charge of all, punishable by death. Hereafter in Mark's Gospel, the shadow of Jesus' death haunts every story until brought into the open by Jesus in 8:27-33; thereafter, his death is the theme that actually governs the narrative. At the point of our passage, the reader sees the dramatic tension in the story: immense popularity in Galilee and forebodings of violent death.

- The interpreter involved in a series of sermons or lessons in Mark would do well to acquaint the listener with this larger unit (2:1–3:6) before focusing upon 2:1-12. At least two major benefits would result. First, one would gain a better understanding of a principle involved in the construction of a Gospel. Major units with common themes are preserved intact, regardless of the literary awkwardness or chronological confusion that may be created thereby. Conflict stories, a series of parables, instructions on discipleship, the passion narrative: these are some easily identified types of materials. Why the present construction? Very likely for functional reasons. The church preserved these stories of Jesus because it saw in his words and deeds the model for its own behavior in situations of conflict as well as worship, evangelism, and instruction of new members. Collections of materials appropriate to such circumstances would understandably be made and preserved.

A second benefit of the procedure suggested above would be that it provided insight into the kinds of conflicts that faced Mark's church and into the ways in which those Christians met those conflicts. Such an exploration of 2:1–3:6 could be most instructive to any church, provided it is thoughtful enough to realize that "being biblical" does not mean deliberately creating those same conflicts in order to give those same answers. However, it is no great strain on the imagination to see the similarity between issues then and now: the word of forgiveness still clashes with calls for law and order and demands for "an eye for an eye"; church rolls turn out to be club rosters when Jesus wants to add publicans and sinners; structures and institutions of society and church can be destructive of the very life they were designed to support; sometimes a human life and a sacred tradition cannot both be preserved unbroken. The centuries have not brought such progress as to remove conflict from the path of discipleship.

We return to 2:1-12. As noted previously, this unit contains two distinct acts of Jesus: he speaks a word of healing and a word of forgiveness. The healing story is complete according to the usual form for such stories: a description of the problem, the healing, the proof of healing in the action of the one healed, and the response of the spectators. But this reconstruction jumps from v 5a, "and when Jesus saw their faith," to v 10b, "he said to the paralytic." The healing story is complete without vv 5b-10a. The crowds are not amazed at the word of forgiveness and the charge of blasphemy, which are, as the story now stands, the most amazing events in the account. The remark that "all . . . glorified God" must have applied only to the healing and stood in a form of the story in which Jesus' critics were not present. In the conclusion the critics disappear as quickly as they appear, even though in its present form the story tells of Jesus' being charged with a capital offense, the very charge that later sealed his death. Finally, the logic that moves from having authority to heal to having authority to forgive sins is rather awkward. Apparently Mark has split one story in order to insert another. Those familiar with Mark's style know his penchant for this literary device. Two notable examples are his insertion of the story of the healing of the woman with a hemorrhage into the story of Jairus' daughter (5:21-43), and his placing of the story of the cleansing of the temple within the account of the cursing of the fig tree (11:12-25).

We have to assume that more is at stake in Mark's split-story technique than simply increasing suspense in storytelling. Mark is a skilled interpreter who relates two accounts in such a way that one story interprets the other. Obviously, in the passage before us, the healing story serves the story of forgiving sin. The central issue for Mark is stated in v 10: "But that you may know that the Son of man has authority on earth to forgive sins." Just as Mark defended the quality of the church's membership by citing Jesus' association with sinners (2:15-17), so he argues for the right of the church to announce the forgiveness of sins by an appeal to the authority of Jesus. Just as Mark justified the church's behavior toward sabbath-keeping on the ground that "the Son of man is lord even of the sabbath" (2:28), so he makes his case here:

"the Son of man has authority on earth to forgive sins" (2:10).

Admittedly, it was difficult to *prove* either that Jesus had such power or that the church's announcement of such forgiveness was efficacious. And when pressed to prove a case, whether for forgiveness or resurrection or some other tenet of faith and life, the church has never done extremely well. But Mark attempts it. As proof that Jesus could speak the word of forgiveness, Mark offers Jesus' word of healing, "Rise, take up your pallet and go home" (2:11). This answer hardly constitutes a convincing argument unless one assumes that healing is more difficult than forgiving sin, and that by accomplishing the former he proves he can do the latter as well. But surely a word of forgiveness is no less powerful than a word of healing. In fact, it would seem to be more powerful.

What we have, then, in this story within a story, is the linking of two announcements. These are two proclamations of the church and not two premises in an argument. The church proclaims that God is at work in Jesus and that his word is powerful to heal and powerful to forgive. According to Mark's narrative, these related issues of who Jesus is and what he can do are centered in the claim of power to speak the word of forgiveness. The scribes sitting there were quite perceptive. It is conceivable that in a healing, factors other than God's power may be at work, but in a case of forgiveness, there is no question. If there really is forgiveness, then it is God who does it, for "Who can forgive sins but God alone?" If the word of forgiveness is effective, then God is present and at work in Jesus, and in the church that speaks in his name.

It just may be the case that the critics of Jesus in this text understood what was at stake much better than some of Jesus' followers. Mark understood, as is evident by his use of one miracle, the healing, to deal with a more profoundly controversial one, forgiving. The critics knew quite well that the issue here was theological. If the word of forgiveness belongs to God, who, then, has a right to speak it?

• The interpreter would be true to Mark and to the issue between Jesus and his critics if he extended this text into the present on the subject of forgiving sins. It is a profoundly difficult but vital matter. Has the church relinquished to psychiatrists and counselors the announcement of forgiveness? Some churches offer no word of forgiveness because there is no sin; others offer none because forgiveness seems to "let people off the hook," condone or encourage unacceptable behavior. Forgiveness seems both the fulfillment of righteousness and the abrogation of righteousness. The statement "your sins are forgiven" speaks volumes about God, God's relation to us, and the nature of the church that would, in Christ's name, continue to make that statement. The church that would be true to its calling must attend to the theology of forgiving lest the word of forgiveness cease as an act of ministry.

In order to pursue this line of thought brought by the text, the interpreter may find it necessary to clear the passage of a popular misuse. Discussions of this text frequently proceed from the position that the paralytic was not physically ill but rather had psychological or spiritual problems. His healing was effected, so this thought goes, by the word of forgiveness. Against this interpretation are two elements in the text. First is the composite nature of the passage, and second is the fact that the word of forgiveness did not heal the man. There was a word of forgiveness and then a word of healing.

A final word about the form of this passage. (See Procedural Guideline 5, p. 22.) By means of the literary device of a split story, Mark has used form to facilitate interpretation. The modern interpreter should try to be just as imaginative. For example, one might describe a church service in which a pronouncement of healing upon the sick was substituted for the sermon. What reactions might there be? The very opposite of the reactions in this text? If so, why?

Mark 8:27-33

Peter's Confession and Jesus' Prediction of His Passion

Two difficulties present themselves as one takes up this familiar passage. First, one is aware of how difficult it is to read Mark and hear *only* Mark. So controlling in church liturgy and doctrine has been Matthew's account with the longer confession, Jesus' approval of the confessions and his blessing of Peter, Jesus' plans for his church, and the explanation of Peter's rebuke of Jesus, that Matthew's voice comes through the wall even when the interpreter thinks only Mark is speaking.

Second, when one does listen only to Mark, one is struck with how difficult this text is. For one thing, there is the unresolved question of whether Jesus knew in advance about his death and resurrection. Some say he knew everything, others that he knew his ministry would bring death but that the church added the reference to resurrection after the fact. Still others regard the entire statement as a post-Easter projection back upon the earthly career of Jesus. Whatever Jesus may have known, the present form of the text is from faith's reflection. No less difficult to comprehend are the three strong rebukes: Jesus rebuked (unfortunately translated "charged" or "ordered" in some versions) the disciples, Peter rebuked Jesus, and Jesus rebuked Peter. Equally thorny is the question of Jesus' response to Peter's confession. Did Jesus accept or reject the title of "Christ?" Why should no one be told, because the title is not right, or because the time is not right? Obviously these and related questions will be central in any effort to interpret. It may be some consolation to us in the process to recall that both Matthew and Luke read Mark and had difficulties also. Matthew dealt with them by elaboration and Luke by abbreviation, omitting altogether the sharp confrontation of Jesus and Peter.

It is clear at the outset that 8:27-33 is a unit and can be

examined as such. The scene shifts abruptly from Bethsaida to the villages of Caesarea Philippi. Caesarea Philippi is beyond Galilee to the north, near Mt. Hermon. But it is an open question whether Mark intends the reader to think geographically or theologically here. Geographically, Caesarea Philippi is away from the swelling crowds of Galilee and is a place for talk with the inner circle. Theologically, Caesarea Philippi is in the opposite direction from Jerusalem, the scene of approaching death. It is Gentile territory, and Gentiles are a concern to Mark. This is reflected by his focusing on Jesus' ministry's being in Galilee, which was regarded by many in Jerusalem and Judea as Gentile territory; in his emphasis on Jesus' rebuke, "My house shall be called a house of prayer *for all nations*" (11:17), and in his story of the confession of faith by a Gentile soldier at the crucifixion (15:39). However Mark wants to be understood, he clearly calls for a shift in thought at 8:27. The same is true at 8:33. The unit is ended, and v 34 introduces a multitude to whom is addressed a collection of sayings which could hardly have been said in one speech. Understandably, however, they are placed here because sayings on cross-bearing and self-denial can reasonably be placed after Jesus' announcement of his own death (although he did not specify it would be on a cross).

But even though 8:27-33 is a distinct unit, it is to be understood in the larger body of material beginning at 8:27 and ending at 10:45. This larger section is held together in a variety of ways. First, it is governed by Jesus' three predictions of his passion. Second, it is set within the larger framework of Jesus, with his followers, moving toward his destination. The recurring phrase is "on the way" (8:27; 9:33; 10:17; 10:32). Third, this material is bracketed by stories of healing the blind (8:22-26; 10:46-52). It can hardly be accidental that Jesus' announcement to his confused and blind disciples about his own suffering and death has been preceded by a story of healing the blind, a healing accomplished with great effort and only after two attempts. Likewise, after the third and final prediction of his passion, Mark relates the healing of blind Bartimaeus, who, upon receiving his sight, follows Jesus "on the way."

In many studies of Mark, 8:27-33 has been regarded as the watershed, the turning point. In popular lives of Jesus of another era, this text was considered the account of Jesus' move out of his "Galilean spring" into his "Jerusalem winter." That is a bit over-dramatic and over-simplified. However, that this is a key passage in Mark's narrative is beyond question.[4] For Mark, its importance does not lie primarily in Peter's confession. There is too much ambiguity in Jesus' response to warrant regarding this as the critical moment in the scene. The confession that Mark regarded as the clear response of faith in Jesus comes nearer the end of the Gospel when a Roman soldier looks at the Crucified One and says, "Son of God" (15:39). Rather, what makes 8:27-33 a central text is primarily its introduction of Jesus' teaching concerning his rejection, suffering, death, and resurrection.

Our text consists primarily of three statements concerning Jesus and three rebukes, arranged in three episodes. These three episodes may be taken up in turn.

The first episode consists of Jesus' question and his disciples' answer (vv 27-28). What is the public opinion of Jesus? Up to this point, those Galileans who have seen and heard Jesus have received one clear image of who he is, even though several titles and phrases have been used. They hold Jesus to be the forerunner of the Messiah (Christ). Like John the Baptist, Jesus has announced the approach of the Kingdom and has demonstrated in powerful word and act the presence of God in their midst. His

---

[4]In all four Gospels this scene is elaborated into major statements about Christ and the meaning of discipleship. See Matt. 16:13-23; Luke 9:18-27; John 6:68-71.

ministry has heightened anticipation, but he has not persuaded the public that he is the fulfillment of their anticipation.

● We should not be to quick to pass judgment upon Jesus' Galilean hearers. We probably read Mark already convinced that Jesus is the Christ, so for us the accounts of his ministry need only to confirm, not to persuade. Moreover, if Jesus' first hearers were bound to an entrenched stereotype of what the Messiah would be like, we can understand that too, since we cherish our own stereotypes of doctors, teachers, ministers, presidents, etc. Jesus, the crowd said, is not the Messiah, but he awakens new hope: he is the one to precede the Messiah. For the Galileans and for ourselves the fact remains that it is easier to believe a Messiah *will* come than that a Messiah *has* come. There is always enough misery in the world to make an announcement that a Messiah *will* come believable. There is always enough misery in the world to make an announcement that a Messiah *has* come unbelievable. The interpreter can at this point, therefore, helpfully show why for some, the second coming of Christ (he *will*) always receives more attention than the first (he *has*).

To sum up this first episode: Jesus asks for the public opinion, the disciples relate what they have heard, and Jesus makes no response.

The second episode consists of the expression of another view of Jesus, followed by a sharp rebuke in the form of a command to remain silent on the subject (vv 29-30). In response to a direct question, Simon Peter (speaking for the group, since Jesus addresses his remarks to all of them) makes it clear the disciples have arrived at a conclusion different from that of the crowds. You are not the forerunner of the Messiah; you *are* the Messiah (Christ). What a temptation to slip over into Matthew here, and to have Jesus say, "Blessed are you, Simon Bar-Jonah!"[5] But our text is Mark, and Mark gives neither approval nor disapproval from Jesus, only the rebuke (charge) that nothing be said to anyone.

[5]R. Bultmann, who usually accepted the priority of Mark, believes that in this case, Matt. 16:17-19 is earlier and Mark abbreviated it. *History of the Synoptic Tradition*, trans. J. Marsh (New York: Harper & Bros., 1963), p. 258.

• The interpreter here must consider the alternatives and decide upon what seems to be *Mark's* meaning. To use this text for probing into Jesus' subconscious and speculating on his self-understanding is hardly fruitful, even though questions tease the mind. Did Jesus so react because he was as yet ambivalent about his role? Was he frightened by the title and its implications? Did he reject it flatly?

It hardly seems correct to say that the rebuke here means Mark and his church rejected the title "Christ" as appropriate for Jesus. Mark uses "Christ" elsewhere approvingly and easily, almost as part of Jesus' name. Note, for example, the opening verse of the Gospel, or Jesus' response at his trial to the question "Are you the Christ, the Son of the Blessed?" (14:61-62). Much more congenial to Mark's whole perspective is an understanding of the rebuke/demand for secrecy which recognizes that prior to the passion, Jesus cannot be properly understood or confessed. Whatever Peter meant by "Christ," whatever his expectations of Jesus, there is no way he could appropriately confess his faith in Jesus until that event had happened which seemed to cancel as incorrect all titles, all confessions—the cross. The passion controls Mark's entire narrative; Jesus is the crucified Christ, the crucified Son of God, the crucified Son of man. Mark will accept all these titles for Jesus *after* they have been reinterpreted by the crucifixion. After the resurrection, when God's vindication of the Crucified One was grasped by the disciples, then they could proclaim it (9:9).

The third episode consists of another understanding of Jesus, in this case followed by an exchange of rebukes (vv 31-33). In this episode Jesus speaks about the suffering, rejection, death, and resurrection of the Son of man.[6] The shockingly new teaching that Jesus begins here focuses, not on the title, but on

[6]Clearly, Son of man refers to Jesus himself, and according to Mark, this was Jesus' preferred self-designation.

the events that will befall him. It is important to notice Mark's elaboration of *suffer, be rejected, be killed* and his quite brief reference to the resurrection. This same proportioning of attention is carried in the remainder of the Gospel, where events leading up to and including Jesus' death form a lengthy narrative while the resurrection material is so sketchy as to seem aborted. This phenomenon in Mark will occupy us in the exploration of 16:1-8 to follow.

> ● At this point the interpreter may sense it appropriate to elaborate upon this particular framing of the passion prediction. One may also reflect on its implication for a church that, quite unlike Mark, minimizes or passes over Good Friday while planning big for Easter, that joins the culture in denying death while talking resurrection, that fails to see there can be no resurrection if no one is dead.

What Jesus says here is not in parables; it is straightforward and clear. In fact, it is clear that Peter rebukes Jesus for a prediction that seems to contradict all the hopes elicited by titles such as "Christ" or "Son of man," as well as by Jesus' own promise that "the kingdom of God is at hand." In a Gospel that rather consistently portrays the disciples as not understanding, Peter's misunderstanding is not surprising. In fact, even after the second prediction of the passion the disciples argue over who is greatest (9:30-34), and after the third, James and John request chief seats in the Kingdom (10:32-37).

> ● It is neither fair nor fruitful to stand upon our post-Easter vantage point and berate the Twelve. Nor does it seem appropriate to enlarge this "blind disciples" motif into the key for interpreting the entire Gospel. The disciples did not see, not solely because they *would* not, but because they *could* not. Therefore, their failure was not final. After the passion, the messenger from heaven would say, "Go, tell his disciples and Peter that he is going into Galilee; there you will see him as he told

you" (16:7). If in Mark, the Twelve represent the church or a portion of the church, then the reader might well identify with them rather than against them, especially if the church has not, even with full benefit of hindsight, taken the cross as a definition of what it means to follow Jesus. Much of the effectiveness of interpretation lies in identification with characters and events in the text. However, the interpreter must beware of an easy identification with Mark's Jesus and of using the occasion to berate the listeners as the modern-day Twelve. It is better to do one's interpreting from the midst of those who listen to Jesus; that is, from among the Twelve.

But even after saying it is not surprising that Peter is portrayed as misunderstanding, one must admit to surprise if not shock at the vigorous exchange between Peter and Jesus, the rebuke and counter rebuke. As was stated earlier, the language of rebuke is the same as that used to silence the demonic spirits who had screamed out knowledge of Jesus as Holy One of God. That this is not simply a coincidence is shown by the fact that Jesus recognizes in the rebuke of Peter the voice of Satan, the very adversary of God. Mark wants the readers to understand that what is happening here is not a theological discussion among associates, not a difference of positions on Christology. What is transpiring here is a fundamental conflict with the powers of evil that would thwart the purpose of God which is to be fulfilled in the passion of Jesus. The language carries the freight of the violent clash between good and evil, God and Satan. The intensity is equal to that of any other scene in Mark in which the powerful presence of God in Jesus is arrayed against the unclean spirits which maim, disease, and destroy. The wrong thinking of Peter is no less crippling than the other diseases countered by Jesus.

• Whether or not the interpreter has paused over episodes one and two, this third dramatic scene must be remarked upon because of Mark's insight into the deceptive and insinuating nature of evil. In the conflict that closes this passage, the locus of satanic power is not in the body of one paralyzed or blind or distraught, not in the attacks of threatening opponents, but in the mind and heart of a disciple and friend. Peter is speaking against violence, not for it; he favors saving life not losing it; he seeks to defend, not to oppose. And yet he is not on God's side. Even the best intentions are so clouded by fear, self-interest, and doubt that penitence, not pride, is the appropriate posture for disciples. Our most charitable projects often conceal a route to the Kingdom that bypasses Golgotha.

Mark 16:1-8
The Women at the Empty Tomb

With Mark's conclusion we end these brief explorations in this Gospel.

That 16:1 begins a new unit is clear from the introductory nature of the opening line, "And when the sabbath was past." In fact, the naming of the women after the previous references to them by name at 15:40 and 47 may be a clue that this story once circulated on its own, or at least in a context different from its present one. But the thorny problem in this passage is the ending. Does Mark end at 16:8? The question must be settled, not by preference, but by an examination of the ancient texts. We are indebted to those scholars who compare, date, classify, and evaluate the more than five thousand Greek manuscripts of the New Testament, quotations of it in the early church fathers, and the early versions of it, in order to help the church make judgments on such matters as this. Different translations indicate to the reader in different ways that there is some dispute about the ending of Mark. In fact, the way the matter is handled in different editions of the RSV underscores the difficulty of the problem. The 1946 edition represents Mark as having ended originally at 16:8, and two other endings are

printed in different type as footnotes. However, in the 1971
editions vv 9-20 are restored to the text, with a footnote
explaining the alternatives. Even so, on the basis of the oldest
and best texts, and because the longer ending contradicts what
Mark has been emphasizing, the ending seems best located at
16:8.[7] This conclusion in favor of the "shorter ending,"
apparently supported by the best evidence, puts a tremendous
burden on the interpreter.

"And they went out and fled from the tomb; for trembling
and astonishment had come upon them; and they said nothing
to any one, for they were afraid." What a strange way to end a
Gospel! It is abrupt; in the Greek text the last word is a
conjunction. Astonishment, fear, and silence are responses
that have appeared earlier in Mark, but the reader anticipates
different responses now that all has come clear in the
resurrection. But this ending seems to turn Easter into an
abortion. The one event that makes sense of the cross, God's
act vindicating the life and work of Jesus of Nazareth, has as its
net effect a frightened silence. Such an ending to the story
stands in contradiction to the natural human response to the
news that God gives life to the dead—a leap for joy, not a
running away in fear. Such an ending stands in contradiction to
the historic practice of the church, which is to shout more loudly
at Easter than at any other time. It is no wonder that Matthew
and Luke, each in his own way, move the story beyond Mark
16:8 to the appearances of the risen Christ and a commission to
the disciples. Both preserve amazement and fear, but these
responses do not control the narrative as they do in Mark.
Neither is it any wonder that scribes added endings (e.g., vv
9-20) which more comfortably "round off" the narrative. Nor is

[7]The details of the arguments concerning the ending of Mark are thoroughly
presented in W. R. Farmer, *The Last Twelve Verses of Mark* (London:
Cambridge University Press, 1974).

it any wonder that some scholars feel that the abrupt and unusual closing line can best be explained by theorizing a longer ending that was lost by being frayed or torn off the scroll. But our task is to understand what we now have, 16:1-8, and to work seriously with the possibility that that is precisely what Mark wrote, no more, no less. How, then, are we to understand it?

The story begins as a simple and beautiful account of an act of devotion by women among the disciples of Jesus. They were helplessly present at the crucifixion and at the burial. Now that the holders of power have had their way and Jesus is dead, the women can at least attend to the body. The reader will notice that the Twelve are not present for this. In the crisis of arrest, trial, and impending death, they had all abandoned Jesus and fled (14:50). In their place are the women. In all of Mark's dark portrayals of the Twelve, this is the darkest. Still, they are not rejected by Christ. This is abundantly clear in the words of the young man in the tomb, "Go, tell his disciples and Peter that he is going before you to Galilee; there you will see him as he told you" (16:7). However, Mark also makes it clear that their restoration and new relationship to Christ is to be facilitated through the good services of these women. Upon receipt of this commission, however, the women flee the tomb, trembling, astonished, afraid, silent. What specific questions are triggered by this story?

First, why is there no record here of an appearance of the risen Christ? In the New Testament, resurrection stories are of two kinds: empty tomb stories and appearance stories (there is no record of anyone actually witnessing the resurrection). Appearance stories are predominant. In fact, the earliest form we have of the Gospel tradition is a recital of Jesus' death, burial, resurrection, and *appearances* (1 Cor 15:1-7). Empty tomb accounts, where preserved, function as narrative preliminaries building toward an appearance. There are two exceptions: Matthew, where the empty tomb assumes a larger role in the writer's effort to *prove* rather than witness to the resurrection; and Mark, where the empty tomb and the word of "a young man in white" are the only testimony to the resurrection. We have to believe that Mark *chose* not to record an appearance of the risen Christ. It must have been Mark's choice, not only because Mark here and elsewhere makes it evident he believed Jesus was raised from the dead, but also because the gospel tradition including accounts of appearances was known as early as Paul (1 Cor 15:1-7), and therefore must have been accessible to Mark. Why, then, did he choose not to use any such accounts?

A possible answer might emerge if one reflects upon the central and controlling image of Jesus Christ in this Gospel. As we have said repeatedly when considering other passages from Mark, it is toward the cross the story moves. It is upon the cross that over 35 percent of the narrative focuses, and it is with reference to the cross that Mark defines discipleship—cross-bearing. That Mark so repeatedly and so lengthily makes this emphasis implies a neglect of it in the church addressed. If the cross were neglected in that community, then perhaps both Christ and discipleship were defined by the resurrection. As we know from the churches of Paul, some Christians certainly minimized the cross and cross-bearing in favor of a glorified Christ and the believer's experience of that glory. If such is anywhere near the truth about Mark's church, then he could hardly afford to weaken his own case by moving his narrative beyond the cross to appearances of the risen and glorified Christ. Such a construction of the story could easily be read as making the cross an ugly preliminary to resurrection, resurrection serving to cancel and erase the significance of the cross. Mark's theology demands that resurrection serve the cross, not vice versa. Resurrection certainly must be affirmed, otherwise the Crucified One is not vindicated. Mark does affirm it. But the affirmation must be in such a form as not to transcend dramatically the crucifixion. Mark does exactly this by two indirect witnesses: an empty tomb and a special messenger. Easter is here, but as the confirmation and vindication of Good Friday.

> ● Notice here how one's appreciation for the theological integrity of the Gospel of Mark helps to clarify the absence of a resurrection narrative. See the discussion of "Integrity," p. 17.

A second question arising out of Mark 16:1-8 is, Why the women's fearful silence? Both Matthew and Luke had access to this story but radically modified it. Both remove the silence, replacing it with the women's carrying out their commission to go tell the disciples. Both retain the fear, but Matthew softens it: "So they departed quickly from the tomb with fear and *great joy,* and ran to tell his disciples" (28:8). Luke, with equal effectiveness, reduces Mark's enigmatic fear that produced silence by pinpointing the cause of their fear. "Two men stood by them in dazzling apparel; and . . . they were frightened and bowed their faces to the ground" (24:4*b*-5*a*). But since Matthew and Luke differ noticeably in interpreting Mark, we have to believe they were not motivated solely by a desire to clarify Mark's meaning, but also to interpret the tradition for their own situations. If so, that is an appropriate task of interpretation, but it leaves the fearful silence for us to unravel. So again, of whom or of what are the women afraid, with a fear so profound as to grip them in silence, a silence so profound as to become for Mark the last word of his Gospel?

It has been argued that Mark stresses the silence of the women because he is answering the question, Why did the empty tomb story become so late a part of the Easter witness? That the Easter witness was first a recital of appearances of the risen Christ and later expanded to include the empty tomb is well documented, but that hardly explains Mark's relating *only* the story of the empty tomb. Told alone, the empty tomb story says that the tomb was empty. Told as a backup story to appearance accounts, it functions as apologetic, marking the church's change in posture from witnessing to proving. Without the appearance narrative, an empty tomb story does not function effectively as either witness or proof. It is hardly convincing to maintain that Mark, who believed the resurrection was the time when the silence should be broken about who Jesus really was (9:9), would set aside that faith and its key significance in his conclusion simply because the empty tomb story entered the tradition late as a result of the women remaining silent for a long time (they must have broken their silence, else how could Mark or anyone have known this story?). Nowhere else in his Gospel does Mark show interest in academic questions, much less enough interest to elevate such a question into the place of primacy of a final paragraph.

Perhaps it would be wise not to search dark corners for an answer, but accept the one that comes front and center: the women are afraid because they are standing inside an empty tomb where Jesus had been laid as a corpse only three days before. They came to anoint a body, but it is not there. Who among us would not be knotted and tongue-tied by fear in such a situation? And then to be confronted by "a young man sitting on the right side, dressed in a white robe": did that increase or decrease fear? Mark describes their response as "amazed." But then, after the young man speaks, the women run in ecstasy, fear, and silence. To have them "afraid" as an immediate reaction to the sight of the young man would have been congenial to other Gospel stories in which fear is the response to the unexpected, unusual, or miraculous. But why is the amazement immediate, and then ecstasy, trembling, fear, and silence the delayed but stronger reactions? Could it be that the young man in white (not an angel appearing as bright as lightning and snow as in Matthew or two men in dazzling apparel as in Luke) was Jesus? That would cause such a reaction, especially after he spoke. Or if they *thought* it might be Jesus, such an "it might be, it can't be" response would account for both ecstasy and fear. But since Mark believed in the resurrection of Jesus, and since appearance stories were available to him, what concern was so strong that Mark refused to move the story forward to at least one appearance, or to the story's natural result, the witnessing of the women?

Consider, in the continuing effort to find the key to Mark 16:8, two possible concerns strong enough to cause the author to stop where he did: one, the germination of faith; two, the dissemination of faith.

The first concern has to do with the generation of faith among the Twelve who are back at square one, having abandoned Jesus and fled (14:50). That necessary kindling of faith will not come by means of response to a miracle. Consistent with the remainder of his Gospel, Mark here makes it clear that faith is generated by the word of Jesus; that is, by a message rather than a miracle. We have already spoken of Mark's reducing the role of miracle in the work of Jesus. If he is addressing a church which set a premium on miracles and experiences of the risen Christ, it is reasonable that Mark does not tell of the Twelve returning to faith by a miracle or an experience of the risen Christ. What Mark has omitted in the closing paragraph is the price he paid to counter the spiritualists (enthusiasts, charismatics) who were trying to turn the church their way.

> ● This is an example of how the interpreter's understanding of the historical context of a document may contribute directly to an understanding of its contents. See Procedural Guideline 2, p. 20.

The time between Jesus' death and his return is characterized by the absence of Jesus but the presence of the Word. That

Word is God's Word of grace and power. In this sense, those who were present during Jesus' earthly ministry are not privileged over those who have a post-Easter faith; both have the same basis for faith: the Word, the message of grace and power. When confronted by that message, the hearer can believe or disbelieve or can hang between. When Mark describes the women responding in ecstasy and in fear, he portrays them as hanging between yes and no. That is reason enough to account for their silence.

A second concern that may clarify Mark's unusual ending is the dissemination of faith. Thus, the frightened silence of the women may indicate, not a cloud over their faith, but a very understandable reticence to proclaim that faith. The fear that stilled their tongues could have been a fear of Jewish authority or Roman rule. The two forces that conspired against Jesus could be expected to move against Jesus' followers, especially if they circulated reports that Jesus was alive. But consider the possibility that the fear that silenced may have stemmed from a sense of the awesomeness of the occasion. Who could speak when running from the God who calls into existence things that are not and who gives life to the dead? If there is any truth in this, then the key to understanding the fearful silence is to look upon Mark 16:1-8 not solely as an ending but as the beginning of a new story. The silence was broken. The very existence of Mark's Gospel and of the church to which it was addressed argue effectively for the new story, or better stated, for a new chapter in the continuing story. By thinking of this text as the beginning as well as the ending, much of the pain of the closing line is removed. And ecstasy, fear, and silence are appropriate to that beginning.

Among enigmas of this last paragraph of Mark, we focus on three. Why no appearances of the risen Lord? Why the frightened silence of the women? And, now, what is meant by the strange mission given by the young man in white to the women: "But go, tell his disciples and Peter that he is going before you to Galilee; there you will see him, as he told you"? The difficulty facing the interpreter here is that a number of meanings present themselves as reasonable and as consistent with the basic themes in this Gospel. For example, the word to the disciples and Peter could be read as a word of grace, an offer to the disciples to be reconciled with Christ, to be restored and reunited in the territory of their major success, Galilee, and removed from Jerusalem, land of plots, conspiracies, arrest, trial, and death. The phrase, "and Peter," if taken as a special extension of forgiveness to the one who had shown himself as confused and cowardly, argues particularly for this commission as a word of grace.

Others, however, have reasoned just as convincingly that the key to v 7 is the word "Galilee." But in what sense is Galilee the key? Perhaps Galilee here represents the Gentiles who are objects of divine concern in this Gospel. Or possibly Galilee is being claimed by the Galilean-Syrian church as the scene, not only of Jesus' ministry, but of his final return, as opposed to the counter-claim found in Luke, which regards Jerusalem as the favored spot. For example, Luke, who has Jesus instruct his disciples, "Stay in Jerusalem," alters Mark's "he is going before you to Galilee" to read, "he told you while he was still in Galilee" (24:6).

Invariably, a consideration of Galilee in Mark 16:7 raises the question whether "going before you to Galilee" refers to a resurrection appearance or to Christ's return in the end time. The issue is whether Mark has no resurrection appearance but promises one, or whether Mark neither offers nor promises any experience of the risen Lord. In other words, does Christ depart at his passion, to return from his place of authority only at the end of time? Matthew interprets Mark 16:7 as a promise of an appearance that occurs in Galilee on an appointed mountain (Matt 28:16-20). In that appearance, says Matthew, Jesus promises to be with them always. But this may not be what Mark intended to say. A better case can be made for Mark's saying that between the resurrection and the final return of Christ, the church cannot expect to be nourished by appearances or by some other form of the presence of Christ. This time between is marked by the absence of Jesus but by the presence of his Word of power.

However, one should not think that "the time between" is in any significant discontinuity with the time of Jesus' earthly ministry. That ministry, as we have seen, was one of manifestations of the power and grace of his Word, and the post-resurrection church still had that Word. Mark joins the two eras (time of Jesus on earth, time of the exalted Christ) in the passage before us: "he is going before you to Galilee . . . *as he told you.*" The exalted (our present line of thought makes "exalted" more appropriate than "risen") Christ repeats the promise made by the historical Jesus (14:28). What Jesus said and what the Lord says are the same.

Therefore, the original and subsequent disciples are not to be differentiated in quality of life and faith because both live and minister by the same word of power and grace. And it just might be that the lack of clear closure, that is, not *fulfilling* but repeating the promise of Jesus, serves a subtle but powerful purpose: to include each generation of readers within this as yet unfinished story. If so, the question is not, "Did the Twelve ever hear and believe this promise of Jesus Christ?" but rather, "Do we hear and believe?"

• Part of the task of the interpreter is to allow the issues and questions within a text to come to the surface. Nothing is gained by pretending they are not there. In fact, dealing with those questions not only clears the way for hearing the text, but often prompts the community to articulate its own questions. They may be very much the same. However, it is fruitless to remain so long in a maze of problems that everyone becomes discouraged and immobilized. Each interpreter will understand the present context and forces bearing upon the lives of the believers, and therefore in each situation will be able to make decisions as to the points of intersection between the text and the listeners.

We have sensed some of the questions and something of the perplexity generated by Mark 16:1-8. However, guided by the principle of intent, one might appropriately bring forward one or two Markan themes into pulpit or classroom. One of these is certainly the accent upon the cross as the key to understanding Jesus as Christ and ourselves as disciples. Mark certainly has a word for those who hide death in euphemisms and use Easter as though it erases rather than vindicates the cross. For Mark the resurrection is God's affirming the way of Jesus, including crucifixion, as the way of God in the world. What could be a more appropriate word to a culture being saturated by "happily ever after" and "how to be healthy and wealthy" religion coming at us daily through television and radio?

A second Markan theme in 16:1-8 is the renewed promise of Christ to his disciples (v 7). In that they had earlier forsaken him and fled, this is a word of grace; in that they are still his disciples, it is a word of commission to continue his work.

In some circumstances, one might determine that a dramatic if not central focus of this text would be the most appropriate intersection with the listener: the awed silence of the women. Their response is profound preparation for the time when they find their tongues and draw their breath in pain to tell the story. Such testimony would surely be more moving and persuasive than the glib chattiness of those witnesses who grab you at red lights and who inquire at grocery counters whether you are saved.

THE GOSPEL OF MATTHEW

A sense of the whole of a Gospel should precede an examination of its parts. It is to be understood, however, that the results of studying particular texts may then modify or even radically alter one's view of the whole. This sense of the whole can be aided by articles about and introductions to the Gospel, but the beginning and point of continued return is the reading of the book itself. Assuming that Matthew has been read in this way, what characteristics of this Gospel are most noticeable?

● One is aided in the identification of these characteristics by comparing Matthew with the other Synoptic Gospels, Mark and Luke, and in particular with Mark, regarded by most scholars as the earliest Gospel. If, as it is by some, Matthew should be regarded as the earliest, some of these observations would have to be substantially revised.

One notices first that Matthew is much longer than Mark, overall. This is even more striking when, upon close reading, one discovers that Matthew, rather than lengthening, actually abbreviates some of the stories in Mark. The extra length is due in large measure to a genealogy and infancy stories in chapters

1–2, resurrection appearances at the end, and large blocks of teachings throughout Matthew.

Second, one is aware of similarities with Mark. Some of these impressions of similarity may actually be cases of our remembering Mark when reading Matthew, and vice versa. But most of these similarities are actually present, and they become vividly clear when the two Gospels are read side by side.[8] About 600 of Mark's 661 verses are in Matthew. Matthew makes modifications frequently, of course, but then he had his readers with their needs just as Mark did. It is not only in amount, however, but also in sequence that the two Gospels are similar. Matthew, in chapters 3–4 and 12–18, is especially close to Mark's order. It is the prevailing, but not unanimous, opinion of scholars that Mark is the earlier and that Matthew is an interpreter of Mark for a different situation. One of the methods an interpreter uses to understand this Gospel is to notice Matthew's modifications of Mark's text. This method will be used in the interpretations that follow.

Third, a quick turning of the pages of *Gospel Parallels* (see Aids for the Interpreter) will show two other phenomena about the content of Matthew. For one thing, some passages are peculiar to Matthew; for example, his particular infancy stories, his resurrection accounts, and several parables (chapters 13, 20–25). For another thing, Matthew shares many materials with Luke that are not present in Mark. Closer scrutiny will reveal that much of this material common to Matthew and Luke consists of sayings of Jesus. Notice, for example, Matthew 5–7 and Luke 6:20-49. This observation has led to the reasonable conjecture that Matthew and Luke had access to a collection of Jesus' sayings. German scholars named this simply *Quelle* (Q),

[8]This may be done by using *Gospel Parallels* (see Aids for the Interpreter) which displays the texts of the Synoptics so that one can readily see relationships among the three.

or "source." That such collections were made we know by the existence of the Gospel of Thomas, a noncanonical Gospel consisting of sayings of Jesus with no narrative thread. These are matters important for the interpreter of Matthew, for in Matthew's modifications of Mark, in passages peculiar to Matthew, and in passages in common with but with some variation from Luke, the interpreter has keys to answering questions about Matthew's intention, his message, and his readers. That this is so, and the means of arriving at such a conclusion, will be made clear as four representative passages from Matthew are interpreted. Anyone who has the opinion that such analyses are too close to the school and too far from the church to be fruitful will surely be convinced otherwise once Matthew's word to the church, as it was then and is now, has been released.

Fourth, the reader of this Gospel is struck by how this Evangelist presents Jesus' relationship to Judaism. This relationship is by no means a simple one. "Book of the genealogy of Jesus Christ, the son of David, the son of Abraham" (1:1) may be the title of the Gospel. It begins with a genealogy from Abraham to Jesus, frames its infancy stories around Old Testament prophecies, tells of revelations through the dreams of Joseph, and climaxes with the rescue of the chosen child from the wicked ruler who slaughters innocent children (recall Moses' infancy). Like Moses, Jesus goes up on a mountain from which he gives God's Word. Jesus' life and ministry fulfill prophecies. Throughout the Gospel, the writer assumes the readers know and reverence Jewish law and that with that tradition there is continuity ("Think not that I have come to abolish the law and the prophets," 5:17). However, there is also discontinuity. Recall the antitheses of the Sermon on the Mount ("You have heard it said . . . but I say to you"), the opposition to scribes and Pharisees (23:13-36), and the many debates over right interpretations of the Law. Like Israel, Jesus was called out of Egypt (2:13-15), but unlike Israel, he was faithful in the wilderness of temptation (4:1-11).

Fifth, a major impression on the reader of Matthew is made by the large amount of teaching materials. These teachings have a number of aims, too many to summarize here. However, to get a sense of what Matthew is doing, one needs to see how Matthew repeatedly clears up Mark's picture of the Twelve as always misunderstanding (cf., e.g., Matt 14:22-33 and Mark 6:45-52, or Matt 16:5-12 and Mark 8:14-21). This "improved" portrait of the Twelve is important for Matthew because they are to continue Jesus' ministry (4:23, 9:25 refer to Jesus; 10:1, 40-42 refer to the Twelve), and to them is given authority to bind and to loose (Matt 16:19; 18:18). Matthew's portrait of Jesus as teacher is also to establish Jesus as the leader like Moses. He is not just a rabbi, but the one whose teachings are authoritative for the Christian community. In fact, on nine or ten different occasions, Matthew describes Jesus as being worshiped, a portrayal of his authority in the church unmatched elsewhere in the Gospels, except for John 9:38. The major content of this teaching also makes it clear that Matthew is concerned to maintain the moral earnestness of the Kingdom. Grace does not abolish obligations. In this focus upon moral and ethical seriousness, Matthew draws upon the Jewish heritage and then warns, "unless your righteousness *exceed* . . ." (5:20). The major reinforcement for these moral demands is not miracles, which play a rather limited role in Matthew, but warnings concerning the final judgment. Time and time again one hears of the outer darkness, weeping and the gnashing of teeth, the fire that is never quenched, the worms that never die. Doors are slammed shut, and pleas for permission to enter go unheeded. The gavel sounds in the final court, and there is no appeal. Grace is present, to be sure, but it is not soft or cheap.

A sixth impression a reader gets from Matthew is that the writer is very often polemical. One can sense this even when the text is vague as to what persons or groups are being opposed. In its milder forms it comes across as an apology for Christianity, an effort to prove or to persuade. Recall, for example, Matthew's account of the voice coming from heaven at Jesus' baptism: *"This is* my beloved Son" (3:17). Both Mark and Luke have *"Thou art* my beloved Son" (Mark 1:11; Luke 3:22). Clearly, Matthew has turned into a proclamation what had been a word of personal experience. Or again, in his resurrection narratives, Matthew argues the resurrection of Jesus and puts the lie to stories of the body being stolen (28:11-15). In its stronger forms, however, Matthew faces opponents and addresses them in no uncertain terms. We noted earlier that scribes and Pharisees were confronted strongly for what Matthew considered misinterpretation and misrepresentation of the Law. But, in what seems to be a battle on two fronts, Matthew also engages false prophets who come among the flocks, wolves in sheep's clothing, apparently champions of a kind of liberty which Matthew sees as lawlessness (24:11-12), eroding the ethical and moral foundations of the community. There persons, sometimes referred to as enthusiasts or spiritualists, practiced a kind of religion using Christ's name for prophesying, casting out demons, and performing wonders (7:15-23). However, their ministries were not approved and would not stand "in that day." The interpreter of Matthew will probably need to help those who have vague, ill-defined, but generally negative reactions to the vigor of the polemics found here. Many in the church have gotten somewhere the notion that in religion there are no hassles.

Since Matthew is longer than Mark, and since the reader does not experience it as a narrative moving swiftly to its close, perhaps a suggestion as to structure would be of help to the interpreter. Several generations of students of the first Gospel have found the analysis of B. W. Bacon helpful (see Aids for the Interpreter). In Bacon's outline the focus is upon the teachings. Viewing chapters 1–2 as preamble and chapters 26–28 as the climax (passion, resurrection), Bacon saw in the center of this Gospel five bodies of teaching from Jesus, the new Moses. These sections of teaching Bacon found by noting the common way they ended: "And when Jesus had finished" (7:28; 11:1; 13:53; 19:1; 26:1). In recent years an alternative overview has been offered by Jack Dean Kingsbury (see Aids for the Interpreter) who feels Bacon's analysis is strained and does not capture the center of Matthew, which, says Kingsbury, is Christology. Kinsgbury offers: Person of Jesus the Messiah (1:1–4:16); Proclamation of Jesus the Messiah (4:17–16:20); Passion, Death, and Resurrection of Jesus the Messiah (16:21–28:20). Either of these outlines could function well for our purposes here. The important thing is to have a grasp of the sweep of the Gospel. The interpreter, after extensive work in Matthew, may venture yet another structure more useful for seeing the intentions of this Gospel and the portraits it wishes to draw of Jesus and his church.

Conjectures about the date and place of writing generally tend toward Syria or Galilee, A.D. 80–90. It is not usually helpful in interpretation to begin with the theories or conclusions of others. One might prefer to reserve any judgment on these matters until after the explorations in the text itself, and then, if so inclined, offer some opinion.

Our selection of texts from Matthew makes a variety of demands upon the interpreter. More important, however, these are passages that can help us understand Matthew's message to the church, then and now.

Matthew 3:13-17
The Baptism of Jesus

Most of the stories in the Gospels portray Jesus acting or speaking, and all who read or hear must interpret from his words and deeds who Jesus is. However, there is a small number of accounts that present Jesus, not through his words or deeds, but through a divine revelation. That is to say, a curtain is drawn back, and to eye and ear God makes an announcement concerning Jesus. These announcements, however vividly described by the writers, are still somehow veiled, because the witnesses seem never fully clear or persuaded at the time as to the nature or meaning of the revelation. The transfiguration of Jesus is such an account, as is the resurrection and, to a certain extent, the birth. The baptism of Jesus, especially as it is told in Matthew, is such a story.

Those who read the Gospels from a purely historical point of view should feel confident that in the baptism of Jesus they have a solid bit of history. True, the accounts of the event reflect in general a Christian interpretation of Jesus' baptism, but the Christian community would not have created a story of Jesus being baptized. Baptism was too consistently associated with sin, repentance, forgiveness, and a new life to have been put into the story. It was already there and had to be interpreted. Among the interpreters in the New Testament, Matthew gives the occasion the most attention with five verses, Mark giving it three, Luke two (and those are in subordinate clauses), and John only an indirect reference.

● But not even Matthew satisfies our curiosity at two points. One, what influences during those long years between child and adult moved Jesus from Nazareth to the Jordan? Two, what was his self-understanding prior to and at the time of his baptism? Since the advent of psychological categories for understanding human

behavior there have been projected into that silence many
readings, often fascinating, sometimes reasonable, but always
unwarranted. We must repeatedly remind ourselves that our task
is not to deal with a topic, the baptism of Jesus, but with a text,
Matt 3:13-17.

Matthew preserves the tradition that existed before him
(Mark 1:9-11), that Jesus was baptized by John in the Jordan
River. Matthew also preserves the threefold drama of
revelation associated in that tradition with Jesus' baptism; the
opening of the heavens, the descent of the Spirit, and the voice
from heaven.[9] What these mean in the tradition and for
Matthew we shall explore later, but that exploration must wait
upon careful attention to Matthew's modification of and
additions to that tradition.

Although there are a number of stylistic changes as the
tradition is passed on, the principal differences are three: the
stated purpose of Jesus' going to the Jordan, the interchange
between Jesus and John, and the voice from heaven. All three
have one thing in common: they are part of Matthew's
apologetic for his Christology. First (v 13), Jesus came to John
in order to be baptized by him. (As in the temptation story [4:1],
Jesus was led by the spirit into the wilderness *in order to be
tempted* by the devil.) Matthew, by means of the purpose
clause, wants it understood that Jesus is with deliberate
intention taking up the way of God. He did not "discover"
God's will, nor did baptism "begin" Jesus' life as Son and
Servant of God. That Jesus went to the Jordan with this purpose
implies that the experience there confirmed, rather than began,
his life as Son of God. In other words, if someone wants to
answer the question, "When did Jesus become Son of God?"

[9]It is not essential at this point to detail differences in the wording among the
three Gospel accounts. These differences are not unimportant, however, and
therefore the interpreter will want to consult commentaries.

with "At this baptism," then Matthew would hardly serve as the supporting text.

The second modification of the tradition, Matthew's addition of the interchange between John and Jesus (vv 14-15), responds to two nagging questions facing the writer: the reason for Jesus' baptism and the relation of Jesus and John. Let us consider the second question first. Even though Christians have neatly arranged John and Jesus as forerunner and Messiah, to their contemporaries this arrangement was not so obvious. John was from Judea, not remote Galilee. He dressed and preached in the tradition of wilderness prophets; he appeared prior to Jesus; he baptized Jesus; he had many disciples, Paul encountering them in Ephesus (Acts 19:1-7) and meeting at least one from Alexandria (Apollos); he was immortalized by death at the hands of a wicked king. And if Jesus began his ministry after being baptized by John, was he a disciple of John? All four Gospels and Acts feel it necessary to respond to the popularity of John and to public opinion about his relation to Jesus. The followers of John the Baptist are apparently alive and well within the area of Matthew's church. One way he handles the problem of claims by John's disciples or confusion between followers of John and followers of Jesus is found in the interchange in vv 14, 15. Whatever the claims of John's disciples, says Matthew, at least John himself knew Jesus was "the mightier one."

As to the reason for Jesus' baptism, Matthew apparently felt the need for some explanation. Mark's silence on the subject seems to indicate neither he nor his church had difficulty with Jesus coming for baptism at the hands of one who preached a baptism of repentance for forgiveness of sin. We do not know Mark's mind because of his silence, but Mark's handling of the tradition certainly created problems for others. It was inevitable that amid developing Christologies the question would have to be addressed: Why was Jesus baptized?[10] Matthew says, "to fulfill all righteousness." In other words, Jesus was doing what God required; he was completely obedient to the will of God. Unlike Israel, who had also been called God's son, Jesus was faithful and obedient, not only in this act, but in the wilderness temptations that follow.

The third major modification of the tradition is found in Matthew's version of the voice from heaven (v 17). The change from second to third person is not insignificant. Mark's having the voice from heaven address Jesus emphasizes the experience of Jesus as consecrated and confirmed as Son of God at the time of his baptism and just prior to launching his messianic work. Matthew, on the other hand, understands Jesus' baptism as the occasion for a public proclamation, pointing others to Jesus ("This is . . .") as Son of God. Matthew's intense desire to prove, to establish, to announce with authority, his message about Jesus is nowhere more evident than in this modification of his source. His respect for Mark's messianic secret, evident in other passages, here gives way to what Matthew saw as the appropriate occasion for a christological announcement.

In view of these uniquely Matthean fingerprints on the story, what can be said of the meaning of Jesus' baptism as presented in this Gospel? Clearly, Matthew presents Jesus as the obedient Son of God. John the Baptist came as a messenger of God's will, and Jesus did not exempt himself from it. He submitted himself not to John but to the purpose of God. In Matthew's eyes, Jesus Christ is doing what Israel failed to do, to be fully obedient to God. Now having come through the water, as did Israel, like Israel he is to face the tormenting struggle of the wilderness. But the reader has no sense of uncertainty as to how

[10]For examples of how accounts of Jesus' baptism became elaborated into testimonies of his divine station and sinlessness, see the notes at the bottom of p. 10, *Gospel Parallels*.

that test will end. All the heavenly signs point to triumph. With
the coming of Jesus Christ to the moment of his ministry,
heaven responds with the voice of approval and announcement
to the world; the heavens are opened (Ezek 1:1) indicating both
divine revelation and the start of a new era of God's relation to
his people; the Holy Spirit is given to Jesus as the power of his
work and word. "Behold my servant, whom I shall uphold, my
chosen, in whom my soul delights; I have put my Spirit upon
him" (Isa 42:1).

This portion of one of the servant passages of Isaiah was
already in the baptism story when Matthew received it, and
even though Matthew alters the heavenly message he does not
remove the servant image. In fact, Matthew later returns to
this passage from Isaiah to explain the behavior of Jesus when
he retreats before strong opposition and continues his quiet
service to those in need (12:9-21). Matthew's portrait of Jesus
as the obedient Son of God finds strong and congenial support
in Isaiah's portrait of the servant of God. (The words "son"
and "servant" are not as distant from one another as it may
seem at first. The Bible treats them as interchangeable
terms.)

A striking aspect of the portrait of Jesus in the baptismal
scene is the hint of Psalm 2:7. Psalm 2 is a coronation psalm, the
king being declared God's son at his enthronement. The
combination of Psalm 2:7 and Isaiah 42:1 joins two qualities not
usually associated: sovereignty and servanthood. The two do
not rest uncomfortably, however, on Matthew's Jesus.

● The interpreter can approach this account of Jesus' baptism
assuming that it was written in a Christian community that
practiced baptism. This means that Jesus' baptism informed the
church's practice and understanding. It also means that the
church's own theology of baptism is most likely reflected in the
way Jesus' baptism is presented; for example, the association of

the receiving of the Spirit with baptism, or the understanding of baptism as entrance into the new age.

If these statements are true, then the church today could fruitfully "listen in" on the understanding of baptism in this text, especially in situations where baptism has become routine and emptied of meaning. Three affirmations about baptism are quite strong in the passage. One, by his baptism Jesus entered into the movement of God's work in the world. The Old Testament (past), John's preparatory ministry (present), and the new age (future) constitute the story in which Jesus enrolls and takes his place. Baptism is not a private act for private spiritual gain, but an acceptance of membership in the historic family of God and a participation in the continuing narrative of God's unfolding purpose. Second, baptism is an announcement. Matthew makes this clear in the case of Jesus. Baptism has a public face; its meaning is not exhausted in discussions of feelings and expressions of devotion. Just as Jesus' baptism was a proclamation, so the church's practice continues to announce something to the world about a God who responds to obedience with the gift of his Spirit and who continues to use his servants to bring in the new age, which has its paradigm in the life and ministry of Jesus. Third, baptism is both coronation and ordination, joining the sovereignty of "You are my child" with the commission, "Behold, my servant" (Ps 2:7 and Isa 42:1). "Servant of God" gives to "child of God" purpose; "child of God" gives to "servant of God" identity.

It is important that the interpreter not empty Jesus' baptism of its meaning by referring to it as an example for Christians. Presenting Jesus' life and ministry as *example* has tended to be subtly destructive of that life and ministry. That much which Jesus did could well serve as an example need not be argued; to say that he did it to set an example is most objectionable. Good examples are set by persons who are not consciously trying to set good examples but who relate to God and to others personally and profoundly.

Matthew 7:21-23
Warning Against Self-Deception

One could question the wisdom of selecting for discussion so brief a passage in view of the overall effort of this book to treat representative materials from all four Gospels. However, these three verses meet most if not all the criteria stated earlier. Two are especially to be noted: this text is representative of much of Matthew's teaching material, and it presents ethical and theological perspectives central to this Gospel.

Matthew 7:21-23 is definitely a unit distinct from the preceding and succeeding paragraphs. Although in general harmony with the themes of hearing and doing which close the Sermon on the Mount, these verses differ from vv 15-20, which cluster around the image of tree and fruit, and from vv 24-27, which focus on the image of a building and its foundation. In addition, vv 21-23 are dominical sayings, which by their very nature have their own integrity and are distinct from the context.

Upon first impression, the text before us seems to be no more or less than Christ's addressing the ageless problem of hypocrisy, that ugly distance between profession and practice. As such, v 21 seems to fit easily with v 20 and also with vv 24-27 that follow. But what about vv 22-23? They represent a noticeable shift in several respects. While v 21 is present tense, vv 22-23 are future; v 21 concerns obedience and disobedience, but vv 22-23 deal with unacceptable forms of discipleship and ministry. Some persons working in Christ's name are rejected in the last day with the charge of being "evil-doers" (workers of lawlessness). In what does their lawlessness consist? Is it what they are doing as prophets, exorcists, and miracle workers, or is it what they fail to do in this form of discipleship? It appears that Matthew has joined two sayings of the Lord (v 21 and vv 22-23) that may have existed separately, the union of the two serving to make a point important for him and his readers.

This possibility finds support when one looks at Luke where parallels to all three verses are found, although in much softer form and with different implications. Matthew 7:21 has its parallel in Luke 6:46. However, Matthew 7:22-23 has its parallel in Luke 13:26-27, an entirely different context. The disjuncture one senses between v 21 and vv 22-23 can therefore best be understood as Matthew's welding of separate sayings. It is also significant that the rejected ones in Luke are those among Jesus' contemporaries who did not believe and who then come too late seeking entrance. In sharp contrast, those rejected in Matthew are disciples who regarded themselves as members of Christ's community and who had been engaged in ministry in Christ's name, performing extraordinary deeds as did Jesus.

● It is this contrast between the two, and not arguments as to whether Matthew or Luke preserves the saying closer to the original, which helps us to see our text more sharply.

Matthew 7:21 carries the theme of obedience to God's will's being the criterion for admission to the kingdom. This is consistent with Matthew's usual characterization of discipleship and with his portrayal of Jesus Christ as the obedient Son of God. As we have noted in passing earlier, and will see in detail when exploring Matthew 25:1-13, the necessity of obedience is so vital and urgent in Matthew's church that he dramatically underscores it with frequent scenes of the final judgment. Verses 22-23 transport the reader to that scene to see and hear the pronouncement of doom upon one particular group of disobedient disciples.

We should pause here to point out what may have already become evident: as it comes to us in Matthew, the saying of the Lord here, especially vv 22-23, presupposes the existence of the post-Easter Christian community. The form of the saying is appropriate to that church and addresses it. The use of "Lord, Lord" here clearly does not convey the common meaning of

"Sir" but is an expression of adoration and praise to the risen Christ. That there are persons ministering in Christ's name implies the activity is subsequent to Jesus' own earthly career. And finally, the picture of Jesus as the one who judges at the end time, the image of the Son of Man come from heaven, not the Son of God on earth obedient to God's will, was surely fixed in the tradition about Jesus after the resurrection.

But what does it mean to say that Matthew is presenting a word of the Lord that bears all the marks of the Christian community which was formed after Easter? Is the saying any less Scripture, any less authoritative, any less the word of the Lord? By no means! This was Matthew's task, to present the word of the Lord to the Christian church of his time and place. His sources brought to him the life and words of Jesus, and his task was to translate that for the believers to whom he wrote. To have formed his Gospel without continuity with the ministry of the historical Jesus would have been completely irresponsible; to have framed his Gospel from quotations and historical reports about Jesus without interpreting them for his reader's own condition would have been equally irresponsible. A Gospel is a retraditioning of the tradition in order to effect a hearing of the Word.

The church Matthew addresses is experiencing the growth of lawlessness (translated in RSV as "evil-doers" in 7:23 and "wickedness" in 24:12). Apparently the source of or at least a stimulant to lawlessness in the church is the active presence of false prophets (7:15; 24:11; 24:24). These false prophets are not easily detected because they wear sheep's clothing, they are within, not without, the Christian community, and their ministries seem so persuasively to bear the marks of Christ. They do what he did: casting out demons, prophesying and working miracles, and they do it in his name.

It is difficult to say with certainty how the ministry of the false prophets produced or contributed to lawlessness. Did they so emphasize special, miraculous activity that they gave insufficient attention to the kind of Christian responsibilities for one another they themselves professed? Or did these disturbers actually preach and promote salvation as freedom from the obligations that pertain to the human community, freedom from earth and for heaven? If we knew they were the kind of enthusiasts who infiltrated the churches of Paul, then we would know better what they were saying and doing.

But whether by default or design, the net effect of the work of those who defined Christianity in terms of exorcisms, prophecies, and miracles was the spread of lawlessness. What Matthew means by lawlessness is disobedience to the ethical demands of life in the Kingdom. That Matthew, following the Jewish custom of avoiding the use of the name of God, says "kingdom of heaven" rather than "kingdom of God," should not cause the reader to equate heaven with hereafter and hence turn all these demands into descriptions of the life yet to come. The expression "kingdom of heaven" is, for this Evangelist, a key term, perhaps a symbol, which will draw vividly to the attention of the church that particular quality of life which is to characterize the Christian community.

• The interpreter will have no trouble recognizing modern counterparts of those who move among believers with claims of mighty works, diverting concern, energy, and money from the implications of the Gospel for basic human relationships. The sale of prayer cloths, pieces of Noah's ark, pocket size crosses that heal, and booklets on how God can make you beautiful, healthy, and wealthy is now a multimillion dollar business. And it is all available right in the living room; no need even to look out the window at a person in need. Matthew does not argue whether or not all those miracles really happened. It is what did not happen that is the issue.

A bit more difficult to define is the positive side of the picture. What is meant by doing "the will of my Father who is in heaven?" One must be careful not to let this expression become a magnet for drawing from everywhere in the Bible all that the interpreter thinks God wants done. Under our mandate to respect the integrity of a document (see p. 17), Matthew should be allowed to flesh out what he means.

At the risk of oversimplification, a strong case can be made that Matthew most clearly and consistently stresses one command: love of neighbor. We can surmise that Matthew is countering forms of false spirituality that claim love of God but which turn the back on persons in need (see 1 John 4:20 and Jas 2:14-17). Even though the advocates of such views are not clearly in focus in Matthew, they are almost visible through the responses this Gospel makes to the conditions in the church. For example, not only is importance given to the command to love one's neighbor (19:19; 22:39), but lawlessness is described as the very opposite, love grown cold (24:12). Recall how much of the Sermon on the Mount is devoted to instructions concerning basic human relationships: a brother takes precedence over offering a gift at the altar; those of the opposite sex are not things to be treated as objects of lust or desire to possess; one does not send away a wife with a paper of divorce; love your enemies; go the second mile; be impartial in all relations so that you may be children of the Father whose gifts of sun and rain reveal no prejudice or revenge but love toward all alike (5:21-48). And, according to Matthew, the last public discourse of Jesus treats this theme in a most dramatic way. The scene is the final judgment, the Son of man has come to his throne to determine the eternal destinies of the human race, and his decisions are beyond appeal. Whether one enters the joy of the Lord or the eternal fire is determined by one's responses during life to one question: What did you do in circumstances where other human beings suffered hunger, loneliness, and privation? (25:31-46).

From the opening Sermon on the Mount to the closing sermon on the final judgment, Matthew's Jesus never mutes or compromises the command, "You shall love your neighbor as yourself." To those who do not, even though they boast, "Did we not prophesy in your name, and cast out demons in your name, and do many mighty works in your name?" he says, "I never knew you; depart from me, you evil-doers."

Matthew 14:22-33
Walking on Water

It has been implied if not stated that a Gospel reveals a good deal about conditions in the particular church to which the account of the ministry of Jesus is being addressed. The significance of this for our present purposes is not simply that we gain information about the early church as well as about Jesus. Rather, the immediate significance lies in our being instructed by the process at work in the text; that is, a church removed from Jesus by time and place is hearing and appropriating the traditions about him. That is exactly what we are trying to do. The passage now before us provides a very clear example of this process.

Matthew 14:22-33 is a distinct unit of material and can be examined as such without violation. It begins with the disciples entering a boat and concludes before they come to land at Gennesaret. It is a story of one night at sea. This is not to overlook the fact that in both Matthew and Mark (6:45-52), as well as John (6:16-21), Jesus' walking on the water is tied to the feeding of the multitude. Whether this means that in the tradition the two stories were joined early or that there is a theological connection is not clear. One thinks of Israel's experience of the sea and wilderness feedings as a background motif, but the understanding of the text immediately before us will probably not be nourished by developing that association in any detail.[11] The part about Peter (vv 28-31) is obviously a Matthean insertion into the story as received from Mark 6:45-52, but this insertion does not destroy the unity of the passage. Luke omits the story entirely.

What kind of story is this? It is not unimportant that this is an account of Christ's power over nature, and that nature is here represented by a sea storm. Upheavals of this sort were evidences to some minds of the cosmic power of sin. "Cursed be the ground for your sake" signified the fallen condition of the created order, and anyone familiar with biblical literature knows that the sea often represents the abode of forces hostile to the good purposes of God. Such a story, therefore, could carry the affirmation of the lordship of Christ over all the created world. This is dramatically sketched in the picture of Jesus standing upon violent waves amid contrary winds, saying, "I am."

But in its present form this is no longer the primary thrust of the story. It is more akin to an epiphany account, more reminiscent of a resurrection appearance. Out of a dark night of fear and helplessness Christ appears to the disciples. They think it is a ghost and are terrified until he reassures them. And the special attention to Peter recalls the testimony that the risen Christ appeared to Peter (Luke 24:34; 1 Cor 15:5). John 21 records an appearance of the risen Lord by the sea of Galilee with Simon Peter jumping into the water (but not walking on it) to go to him. But whatever may be the literary or historical or theological relationship between these accounts and the text before us, they are not sufficiently in the foreground, nor even clearly in the background, to be the basis for interpreting what Matthew is saying.

[11]In John 6, the "manna in the wilderness" is developed into a "bread from heaven" christological theme that argues Jesus' superiority over Moses.

Matthew has made two major changes in the story as received from Mark 6:45-52: the insertion of the story of Peter and the radical alteration of the ending. These two Matthean touches make it clear that the writer is weaving into a story set in Jesus' ministry a word of judgment and grace for the church. That the narrative in its present form is a post-Easter church story is evident in the closing scene in which the disciples worship Jesus as Son of God. Such worship of Jesus was not a pre-Easter phenomenon. This scene is paralleled in the resurrection story at the close of Matthew. There, too, the living Christ and Lord of the church comes to his disciples, and, as in the present text, there is that familiar mixture of doubt and worship (28:16-17). Similarly, there is in both accounts the initial response of fear. In other words, fear, doubt, and worship characterize the response of the disciples to the Christ who comes to them as he promised. In response to their fear, he says, "I am he" (v 27). In their doubt, they say (in the person of Peter, who voices the courage and fear, the faith and doubt of the group), "If it is you" (v 28). Finally assured, they say, "You truly are" (v 33).

Imagine for a moment that this story appeared in the Gospel as a post-Easter story, that it constituted one of the occasions of Jesus' appearing to his disciples. Were it so located, it would be much easier to understand. The night has been long, and as dawn approaches they are near despair. Across the water not subject to laws of time and place, the risen Lord comes. As a ghost? No, but so they think, becoming shocked and frightened. Then there is the word of assurance. Is that enough to reestablish faith? Almost. "If it is you," confirm it by an authoritative command. He does. Is that enough? Almost. But it is only his presence in their midst that fully and finally elicits confession and praise.

If, then, the narrative moves so naturally as a post-Easter encounter with Christ, how are we to understand its present location in the earthly ministry? One answer could be that it actually occurred at this time in his ministry; but if so, it is striking that the disciples who are pictured here as confessing and worshiping are portrayed in subsequent scenes as though this had never occurred. It would be a more meaningful answer to say that the Gospel writer's reflections upon the power and presence of Christ did not respect chronological distinctions of pre- and post-Easter experience. Jesus is the living Lord, and the living Lord is Jesus; what he is and does, he was and did. The writer would have regarded it especially important to insist that the power of the presence of Christ was not confined to past or to future; he is truly and effectively present now, whether that "now" be in the time of the Twelve, or of Matthew's church, or (we might add) of our own. Therefore, to call this story a "misplaced resurrection story"[12] is not helpful. Saying it is "misplaced" presupposes a historian's chronological interest, but this was not the interest of the writer. We must remember that the document before us is a Gospel, a proclamation of Jesus Christ to the believing community. Proclamation does not and cannot take place until the transcending significance of a word or act is seen and expressed in such a way as to be as present, as meaningful, as available to the hearer as to those who first saw and heard. This is not to play games with history; it is simply a refusal to be a victim of it, a confession of faith in him who both entered history and transcended it. Matthew's way of narrating, his interweaving of past and present, persuades the reader that he understood that transcendence quite well. In so doing, however, he sometimes leaves two readers unsatisfied: the pure historian seeking only the facts and the pure allegorist who is uninterested in history.

[12]This phrase is my own to summarize the discussion of E. Schweizer, *The Good News According to Matthew* trans. D. E. Green (Atlanta: John Knox Press, 1975), p. 321.

• The interpreter will want to give appreciative attention to some small but not unimportant details in the narrative.

The entire scene, set between a crowd (14:12-21) and a crowd (14:34-36), involves only Jesus and his disciples. These are rare moments in the Gospels and provide both writer and reader occasions for glimpses inside the church to ascertain its nature, its faith and failure, the quality of its life. The fact that many find it easy to preach on this text testifies to Matthew's having already seen in the story as he received it an analogy of the church in the world as a boat in a storm. The story is further shaped by this evangelist into a clearly discernible lesson or sermon. Note the movement: the disciples are in a boat without Jesus; a storm arises, overwhelming and threatening them; Jesus comes, bringing first fear and then assurance; the disciples, in the person of Peter, are now emboldened to face the storm and overcome it as Jesus did, and the venture almost succeeds; Jesus again rescues from the storm, which ceases when he enters the boat; the disciples now worship him as the Son of God. The story takes place between occasions of feeding and healing, in an interim when the disciples were under orders (14:22) from the Christ who had demonstrated in their presence that he cares and that he is able to provide. Ordinarily the miracles of Jesus are for others, for those who come in need seeking his help. The disciples are involved in such miracles usually as witnesses and sometimes as helpers, as in the feeding. But in our text these disciples are recipients, beneficiaries of a miracle, a very unusual event in the Gospels.

• Perhaps the disciples of Jesus are thereby reminded that they, too, have needs, that they, too, still have fears, doubts, and inadequacies, that they are in reality disciples on the way to becoming disciples. This word needs to be said to Christians who have been made to feel guilty for the lack of a "born again" experience that is final, total, and perfect.

Matthew's view of the inadequacy of the disciples is not that of Mark. In Mark, here (6:52) and repeatedly elsewhere, the disciples fail to understand, and that failure is not softened or relieved as Mark's narrative progresses. In Matthew, their problem finds its most frequent description and judgment in the words of Jesus, "You of little faith" (8:26; 14:31; 16:8; 17:20). They are not without faith; they have insufficient faith. This is dramatically illustrated in the inserted story about Peter, a vignette that has been placed between a description of the disciples as fearful (vv 26-27) and a description of them as confessing and worshiping Christ as Son of God (v 33). Between fear and faith is Simon Peter, in this episode as in others the voice and heart to the group, "If it is you" he says, with commingled doubt and faith. He walks and he sinks, he trusts and he fears. But as he often does in Matthew (and does not in Mark), Jesus nourishes the "little faith" to the point of confession and praise.

The believing community, says Matthew, continues to experience the power of Christ's presence. That presence comes as judgment upon fear and insufficient trust, but that presence also responds in grace to fear and doubt.

Matthew 25:1-13
The Parable of the Ten Maidens

We come now to a parable, the form of teaching most commonly associated with the ministry of Jesus.

● Because of its importance ("He said nothing to them without a parable," Matt 13:34) and its frequent occurrence in the Synoptic Gospels, the interpreter would do well to spend some time understanding the parable as a literary form before attempting to interpret any one parable in particular.[13] See Procedural Guideline 5, p. 22.

Parables were commonly used by sages and rabbis in Israel, sometimes to clarify, sometimes to raise a question. Parables are brief narratives ranging in length from one sentence to several paragraphs, and ranging in complexity from childlike clarity to riddles. They draw upon observable nature or common human experiences and part of their appeal is the listeners' easy recognition of and identification with events and characters. As vehicles of clarity, parables are often elaborated proverbs, but on the lips of a prophet a parable can draw the listeners into the story, unaware that they may suddenly come under the judgment of the truth of the story. In such uses of the parable, the story usually proceeds along familiar and predictable lines only to take an unexpected turn, surprising and ensnaring the hearers. This turn in the story offers a new perspective, opens a new vista, and therefore, by its offer of an alternative, forces listeners to rethink an issue or a relationship. Think of the many parables of Jesus that "trapped" the hearers into radical reconsideration of life and God and the Kingdom: a party for a prodigal, a tax collector justified, a one-hour worker paid a day's wage, rewards for servants who had taken big risks with the master's money, the smallest seed making the biggest tree, a shepherd leaving ninety-nine sheep in the wilderness while he goes looking for one. Such parables are especially effective for communicating the surprise of grace to persons who have been busy calculating the rewards and punishments of the Kingdom.

However, it is very important to keep in mind that not all parables have the twist that surprises with the gift of grace. This

[13]For a survey of various approaches to parables, see Norman Perrin, *Jesus and the Language of the Kingdom* (Philadelphia: Fortress Press, 1976).

"surprise ending" type has achieved great popularity in recent years, and deservedly so. These powerful stories have been too long reduced to harangues and exhortations about what everyone ought, must, and should do, or else lost in improper spiritualizing, which sought meanings that were never intended. But some parables, indeed some of the parables of Jesus, offer no surprises. Their story lines follow the straight course of cause and effect as naturally as what is reaped comes from what is sown. These convey a sense of justice just as the others carry a sense of grace. One would anticipate at least some such parables in Matthew for, as we have learned, this Gospel is concerned to recover the moral and ethical earnestness of the Christian life. Stern demands concerning the superior righteousness rather than frequent offers of grace impress the reader of this Gospel. In fact, some interpreters of Matthew have theorized that perhaps a source of ethical erosion in his church was a misunderstanding of grace similar to that which plagued Paul's churches. But whatever the sources, conditions are such as to elicit reminders of judgment and final accountability to God. In terms of parables, this means straight stories with predictable conclusions, wages and just deserts, not gifts and parties.

Matthew is certainly not without parables of surprising grace. However, one must also note the presence of some parables that reflect just deserts rather than free grace. Indeed, if both types were not present, neither type would have any meaning. Grace functions in a climate of responsibility and demand. Where every word is a word of grace, there is no grace. And conversely, where every word is a word of demand and accountability, there is finally no responsibility, only despair. Interpreters of Jesus' parables should not pick and choose favorites with happy endings; they should reflect the balance achieved by the Gospel writer.

All these comments have as their immediate purpose preparation to hear a parable that moves straight from cause to predictably painful effect: the door was shut and would not be opened.

• Two early steps are necessary in interpreting parables in the Gospels. First, the parable itself needs to be isolated from the commentary of the writer who uses it. As a general rule, the parable is seldom altered internally, but rather is passed along in the tradition as a literary unit, its form being so essential to its function that it successfully resists serious modification. Commentary, therefore, is added by way of introductions and closing comments. Matthew's usual pattern is to offer brief comments at the close, often in the form of a proverb, such as, "the last shall be first and the first last." The task of isolation is for this reason not usually difficult. Second, the interpreter has to decide whether to concentrate upon the parable itself as it is preserved and now isolated from the context or to focus upon the Gospel writer's understanding and use of parable. An interpretation of the parable in isolation would be an exercise in seeking to reconstruct its original setting and function in the ministry of Jesus. In other words, what did Jesus mean by this story? Studying the parable in its present setting would be interpreting Matthew's interpretation. But whatever one's primary concern in the investigation, the isolation of the parable is essential in order properly to identify what is parable and what is commentary. The point is, the interpreter should not move around in both parable and commentary as though it were all from Jesus or all from the Gospel writer.

Matthew 25:1-13 contains a parable found only in Matthew. (Luke 12:35-36 and 13:25 contain fragments of parables somewhat similar.) Commentary on the parable by the writer consists primarily of the general context in which it is placed, the introductory word "then" (25:1), and v 13. The word "then" is typically Matthean and functions to tell the reader that the story about to be read concerns the future, and in particular, that time in the future which governs all the discussion from Matthew 24:36 through 25:46: the certain but unknown final day and hour. The exhortation to "watch" in v 13 is obviously commentary that applies to this entire section, but not particularly to this parable of the maidens. In this parable it is not watchfulness that is being enjoined; after all, all ten maidens slept (v 5). The issue here is preparedness in the face of uncertainty.

As to the parable itself, there is much debate whether it comes from Jesus or is entirely the creation of the early church, perhaps Matthew himself. There are basically three arguments that it is totally an early church story. First, it concerns the delay of the day of judgment, and even if Jesus did teach concerning that day, he surely would not have taught its delay. The early church, on the other hand, certainly had to deal with the delay of the Parousia (second advent of Christ). Second, the marriage practices depicted do not correspond to our knowledge of such occasions. Therefore, the story must have been fabricated to convey spiritual or transcendent truth; in other words, it would be an allegory. Third, the story is to be understood as an allegory of the Christ as the heavenly bridegroom coming to earth to receive his bride, the church. Those who regard this as a parable of Jesus acknowledge that it has, in the hands of Matthew, been "futurized" to address the problems related to the delay of Christ's coming. Originally it probably dealt with the urgent call to the disciples for preparedness in view of the Kingdom's having come upon them. As to the claim that the wedding scene does not correspond to historical information, the response is simply that we lack information about first century weddings in that culture and therefore cannot prove or disprove the story's accuracy. As to the story being an allegory of the heavenly bridegroom coming for his bride, the problems

are obvious. Since the story lacks a waiting bride to represent
the church, the ten maidens are treated as the bride—the
church—partially faithful, partially unfaithful. Obviously,
pressing the story so as to have the groom's attendants be the
waiting bride makes for an awkward allegory. One can see how
with a little alteration the story could become allegory, and so it
did later. It seems more reasonable, however, to understand
the story as it now stands as a parable of Jesus modified in the
church's retelling to address the issue of the Parousia.

As we have received it from Matthew, the story clearly
depicts the future, that time to which Matthew points with the
opening word, "then." And what does the parable tell the
reader concerning that day and hour? It is not a message to the
effect that the time is short and even now the signs of its being
near are evident. On the contrary, the dramatic center of the
parable is the expression, "the bridegroom was delayed." That
delay created the crisis; that delay was the circumstance about
which some proved wise and some foolish; that delay triggered
the series of events ending in the final exclusion of those
unprepared.

When one looks at the larger context it is even more evident
that the delay of the end time is the key to the story. This
parable is one of three bearing this theme. In the parable of the
faithful and wise servant occurs the statement, "My master is
delayed" (24:48); in the parable before us, "As the bridegroom
was delayed" (25:5); in the parable of the talents, "Now after a
long time the master of those servants came" (25:19). In three
successive stories Matthew addresses a problem facing his
church: the adjustments that are appropriate to a recognition
that the Parousia has been delayed, perhaps indefinitely.

We do not know how widespread and how intense the
expectation of an imminent return of Christ was. We do not
know to what extent that expectation was a prime motivating

factor in the quality of life and the sense of mission in the early church. It could be surmised, however, that such an expectation lay at the heart of the faith of many, because New Testament writers devote so much attention to the problems created by "the delay" and instructions about life in the world in the meantime.

In the face of whatever problems the delay was creating in the church, Matthew absolutely refuses to abandon eschatological expectation. Whatever may be the nature and extent of present realizations of the Kingdom, the future remains as the time of completion and final reckoning.

● The comments above have focused on the parable as Matthew interpreted it for his situation. If the interpreter can isolate the parable as Matthew received it, perhaps as Jesus told it, then it would be appropriate to develop Jesus' teaching concerning the presence (not the future coming) of the Kingdom as signaled by his ministry. That is to say, how does one respond to the *arrival* of the bridegroom? However, in view of so many current voices proclaiming the end of the world and the imminent return of Christ, it may be wise to hear Matthew's word in this text, and indeed, in the whole of chapters 24–25. Rather than rehabilitate the doctrine of an impending end, the Evangelist does the opposite; he presents a theology for the "delay," for the ongoing life of the church in the world. Since some modern announcers of the final return of Christ have clearly abdicated all responsibility for the life of this world, the message of this text needs to be heard. The maidens who calculated an immediate arrival of the bridegroom were the ones in trouble. Accurate or inaccurate calculating is not at all the issue. The issue has to do with responsible behavior *in the meantime*. The coming of the bridegroom does not make some wise and some foolish; it merely reveals who has been.

THE GOSPEL OF LUKE

For the reader who has been following closely, the preceding work in Mark and Matthew could have the effect of dulling the appetite for a third Gospel which may seem to be yet another account of the same story. However, this concern vanishes with the reading of the Gospel of Luke itself. Perhaps some reflections upon the experience of the entire Gospel will aid understanding without robbing us of discoveries to be made in the particular texts selected for investigation.

To begin with, any reader is bound to be impressed by the extent of what this writer has produced. The author of this Gospel is also the author of Acts, and these properly constitute a single, two-volume work.

• Our task here is to experience the literary and theological integrity of the Gospel of Luke (see the discussion of "Integrity," p. 17), and this requires some attention to the Book of Acts as well.

In a way it is regrettable that the Gospel of John stands between Luke and Acts. This causes many to read the Gospel of Luke only in relation to the other Gospels, and Acts only in relation to the career of Paul. As a result, many people overlook the continuity in the story of Jesus and the early church which Luke has sought to emphasize, as well as the parallel he draws between the life and work of Jesus and the life and work of the church, even while providing separate and distinct portraits of the time of Jesus and the time of the church. Naturally, the sheer volume of material will prompt the interpreter to allow more preparation time in advance of presenting lessons or sermons on Luke, since failure to get an overall perspective first would cause each lesson or sermon to be haunted by uncertainty and detachment. The size of the task is in itself both a challenge and a promise of rich returns. Luke-Acts constitutes well over one-fourth of the New Testament (142 of the 523 pages of New Testament now before me), the greatest contribution by volume of any single writer.

Moreover, the Gospel of Luke presents us with much new material. Luke constructs his Gospel using only one half his stones from the old quarries of Mark and Q (that is, material common to Matthew and Luke which is not in Mark). The other half of his material, whatever its source, is seen by the reader for the first time in Luke. Noticeably new materials are Luke's stories about Jesus' birth, infancy, and childhood, and his resurrection narratives. He also has a number of parables not present in Matthew or Mark. And even the old stones have been so reworked and rearranged as to give the clear impression of a new building.[14]

This writer has worked his sources into a masterful literary whole. One may even speak of the literary "beauty" of Luke's birth and childhood stories, of his parables of the prodigal, the Pharisee and the publican, the widow and the judge, the good Samaritan, the rich man and Lazarus, and others, and of his

---

[14]Commentaries will debate how "new" the building is. For example, does Luke use Mark's broad outline, or does he follow another, perhaps his own?

story about walking with Christ on the way to Emmaus. But the extraordinary beauty of these materials need not detract from their *power* any more than the recognition that many Old Testament prophetic oracles are poetic diminishes their impact. In fact, the enthralled reader is soon the addressed and convinced reader.

In this same vein it should be said that the *quality* of the literature in no way erodes the reader's experience of these two volumes as a kind of historical writing. In that culture historical narratives were often the work of rhetoricians. With his sense of God's purpose providing the continuity from creation to the close of the story he wishes to tell, Luke weaves together the history of God's people and secular history. Luke tells not only of Abraham, Isaac, and Jacob, but of Adam and of the God who "made from one every nation of men to live on all the face of the earth" (Acts 17:26). He writes not only of Jesus and the Twelve, but of Augustus, Tiberius, and Claudius; not only of Bethlehem and Jerusalem, but of Athens and Rome.

But in this grand understanding of God's achieving his purposes through Caesar Augustus no less than through Simon Peter, Luke in no way minimizes the roles of Israel, of Jesus, and of the church. Each of these three "eras" is positively viewed, having its own chapter in the total narrative of God's plan to bless with salvation all the nations of the world.[15] The key event is the work and person of Jesus of Nazareth in whose name repentance and forgiveness of sins are to be preached to all people. In his unfolding of this story Luke seems to be concerned solely that his readers understand "the things which have been accomplished among us" (1:1) and not that the church of his day return to the glory of the past. Luke is not

---

[15]This view of Luke's narrative as falling into three periods: that of Israel, of Jesus, and of the church, is presented in detail by H. Conzelmann, *The Theology of Saint Luke* trans. G. Buswell (New York: Harper & Bros., 1961).

calling for a return to "the good old days." Each time has its own appropriateness in the purpose of God, and that includes the time of the reader of this Gospel.

Many writers refer to Luke's history as "theological" history, and this is a significant qualifier. It refers to the fact that Luke is not just concerned with what happened, with events accessible to any historian, but with what *really* happened. Luke interprets events in the light of his central affirmation that God is at work in and through persons, nations, institutions, and laws. He tells his story, therefore, from this standpoint, whether the particular event be a decree of Caesar Augustus, the death of Judas, or the release of a missionary from prison. Since it is God who is achieving his purpose in history, a visit by an angel and a decision by a Roman governor are told with equal ease and filled with equal importance. In fact, since God is also Creator, even the natural order testifies to him who has never left himself without witness (Acts 14:17).

To speak of Luke's history as theological is also to be reminded that God, not Christ or the Holy Spirit, is the central subject. If this sounds unusual it may be because many Christians have so focused on Christ or the Holy Spirit that they forget it is God who sent Christ and who sends his Holy Spirit. "God" tends to be the neglected subject among us. But not so with Luke. Throughout the Gospel and Acts it is God who acts, who is praised, who visits his people, who sends the Christ, who raises up Jesus, who gives the Spirit, who will judge the world, and who is Savior. Luke closes his Gospel with Jesus' disciples in the temple blessing God, a scene often repeated in Acts.

This theological unity, which Luke sees permeating history from the beginning to the present, also influences his angle of vision on Judaism and the Old Testament. He sees no radical discontinuities between Judaism and Jesus or between Jesus and the church. True, Israel has resisted God and has acted "in ignorance" against the Lord of Glory, but throughout the story, God is faithful. God has not changed his mind. What he did in Jesus was no more or less than what he promised in the Scriptures; what he is doing in the church (proclaiming repentance and forgiveness of sin to all nations) is no different from what was promised to Abraham and repeated by the prophets. Neither Jesus in the Gospel nor Paul in Acts represents a departure from what God sought to do with Israel. Jesus was circumcised on the eighth day and dedicated in the temple at six weeks, made a pilgrimage to Jerusalem at age twelve, was customarily in the synagogue on the sabbath, and was preaching in the temple in his last hours before death. Luke's portrait of the apostles and Paul does not depart from this. God is faithful; he has not changed his mind; he is fulfilling his purpose, not abandoning it.

This emphasis on the continuity of God's acting in history should never be forgotten by the interpreter of Luke-Acts. It will prevent, for example, certain popular misrepresentations of Luke's ideas about Judaism. Under the oft-repeated rubric, "Luke is the Gentile Gospel," many sermons and lessons thoughtlessly contrast Luke with Matthew, as though Matthew tied Christianity to Judaism and Luke did not. It is true that Luke, unlike Matthew, does not usually make direct "as it is written" use of the Old Testament. He is often allusive and indirect, sometimes patterning a story about Jesus or the church on a scriptural narrative without making any explicit reference to it (e.g., Luke 7:11-17 and 1 Kgs 17:17-24, or Acts 5:1-11 and Josh 7:10-26) Such allusions may be easily missed by persons not familiar with the Old Testament. But when one carefully examines Luke it becomes clear that Luke is in no way second to Matthew in establishing continuities between Old and New. In fact, it is in the Scriptures of Israel that Luke finds his good news for the Gentiles. Because God's promises are present there, Luke insists that the Scriptures are adequate for creating and sustaining faith. As father Abraham said to the rich man in torment who wished to have Lazarus sent back to earth to warn the rich man's brothers, Jesus said, "If they do not hear Moses and the prophets, neither will they be convinced if someone should rise from the dead" (16:31). Scripture (what we call the Old Testament) is so central to his theology that Luke describes the primary work of the risen Christ as interpreting for his disciples the witness of the Law, the Prophets, and the Psalms (24:27; 24:44-47).

So rich and suggestive are the materials gathered and interpreted by Luke, so persistent are certain themes and motifs, that no single hypothesis as to his purpose includes all of them. Some scholars are convinced Luke wrote the first Christian apology, a defense of Christianity before Rome. The prologue to the Gospel (1:1-4) certainly has that flavor, and Luke consistently shows not only the innocence of Jesus and Paul in the eyes of Rome, but also Rome's protection of Christian leaders from mob action. However, most of the Gospel and much of Acts seems to be unconcerned about a legal defense of the faith. And so others have argued that Luke's purpose was to show how and why a movement within Judaism had become, by Luke's time, primarily Gentile. Is that hypothesis served by the contents of the two volumes? Or does Luke present Christianity historically as a counter to spiritualizing groups (Gnostics?) that were negative toward the world and history? Or perhaps the delay of the Parousia (second coming) persuaded Luke that the church needed a sense of history in order to have a clearer self-understanding and to be able to reformulate what it meant to live as an institution with a mission in the world. Then again, it has been theorized that in the face of rising heresies, it was Luke's purpose to present a proper understanding of Jesus, to identify the group of apostles to whom he gave authority to continue his work, and to establish the primacy of Jerusalem as the mother church with which mission churches were to be in accord.

• For any of these views, and for several others, strong support can be gathered from the text of Luke-Acts. But none of these theories should shorten the interpreter's own fresh exploration of the material. A new reading of the text may discover constellations of evidence that argue for an entirely new direction in pursuit of Luke's purpose or purposes. Sometimes a study of the text is aided by a simple outline of its contents, an outline that one may modify or reject as one increases in knowledge of the text. One such outline is as follows:

    1:1-4   Prologue
    1:5-2:52   Birth and Childhood of John and Jesus
    3:1-9:50   Ministry of Jesus in Galilee
    9:51-19:27   Teaching of Jesus on the Way to Jerusalem
    19:28-24:53   The Days in Jerusalem

Regardless of whatever view of Luke's purpose the interpreter subscribes to, he will be left with one clear impression: an early Christian writer has presented the story of Jesus and the story of the church as one continuous narrative, as a kind of history. To be sure, it is history interpreted theologically, in order that the reader might know what God was doing in and through the events which transpired, but it is history nevertheless. We have no other work quite like it in the New Testament, but was this an entirely new phenomeon in Christian writing? Did it have antecedents? What sources were accessible to Luke, and how did he go about his task? Or are these questions with no available answers? Fortunately for us, in a preface to his Gospel, Luke discusses his work as a writer. To that brief paragraph we now turn for our first exploration of this Gospel.

Luke 1:1-4
The Prologue

Were we selecting only passages that are completely representative of each gospel, we would pass this one by; there is nothing like it in the remainder of Luke. In fact, this prologue is unique in all the Gospels. But it does qualify for examination because it is a text of central importance for understanding this writer.

Luke 1:1-4 consists of a simple sentence, written after the manner of the classic rhetoric of the time.[16] The style is clearly intended to impress a cultured reader who is accustomed to such courteous and ceremonious introductions. The reader is approached with respect and allowed to be a partner in what follows, rather than surprised or shocked into giving attention to the matter to be discussed. The writer has distanced himself from the entire enterprise and thus is able to be aware of himself as writer, Theophilus as reader, and of the manuscript before him. To our knowledge, the Gospel of Luke represents the first effort of a Christian writer deliberately to attempt to present the message as good literature. In other words, there is the Christian story; now there is a story presenting that story.

It seems appropriate to interject two brief reflections upon Luke's apparent concern for literary quality. First, the church has not always had unanimous praise for artistic expressions of the faith. In spite of the fact that quality in communication not only honors the message but enables it to reach ears that would otherwise be inattentive, there remains firmly entrenched in some areas of our culture the notion that truth is necessarily crude and without finesse. Many voices have warned the faithful to be wary of rhetoric and its power to enthrall and

[16]For examples of such style, read the preface to *Ecclesiasticus* and the introductions to Josephus' *Wars* and *Antiquities*.

beguile, implying that sincerity and integrity belong only to the awkward and poorly prepared. Not surprisingly, therefore, Luke as literature has often been more appreciated outside the community of faith than within it.

Second, within this material addressed specifically to readers with culture and taste, there is conveyed a deep concern for the poor and the disenfranchised of the earth. Does there lie in this combination some contradiction or perhaps insincerity in Luke's expressions of care for the poor? Not at all. Genuine passion for the oppressed does not necessarily come only from one who is also oppressed. The poor and downtrodden do not often write in behalf of the poor and downtrodden; food and clothing, not literature, occupy mind and hand. Efforts in behalf of the have-nots are often made by those who have the time, means, and ability to help. Luke may be such a person. If his writing is an adequate introduction to him, then he does not fit in the popular portrait of early Christians as a deprived and unlettered lot. On the other hand, we are not justified in seeing in Luke clear proof of the general upward mobility of the Christian community.

Let us turn now to the content of the prologue. What is said or implied that will help the reader of Luke-Acts better understand and experience the accounts that follow?

Luke's opening lines make the reader aware of the passing of time and emphasize how critical that often unnoticed fact is for the life of a community or institution. The time of the author is removed from the time of "the things which have been accomplished among us" (v 1), those things being, as far as the Gospel is concerned, "all that Jesus began to do and teach" (Acts 1:1).

● Notice here how an appreciation of Luke-Acts as a single, two-volume work enhances the interpreter's understanding of each volume. The opening verses of Acts look back on the Gospel of Luke.

The writer is aware of that distance but is persuaded that the record of the beginning is of value and must be, not simply preserved, but told. Apparently the loss of that record would be irreparable, and perhaps fatal, for the Christian community. He indicates no desire to reproduce in his own time and place the life and structure of the Jerusalem church. Respect for the integrity of the past insures that it will best serve the later generations of Christians who wish to know the origins and destiny of the Christian community.

Luke sets himself to the laborious task of carefully tracing out that past. The tradition from eyewitnesses and ministers of the word had to be investigated (v 2), not because it had not been recorded by others, but perhaps because it had been recorded by so many. Many narratives were already in existence. We know one of them, Mark, but eventually at least fifty Gospels were written. Why add another? That Luke does his own research, that he wants to record the events "in order," and that he wants to give his reader "certainty" concerning matters that were to some extent already known, all combine to argue that Luke regarded the existing narratives as incomplete, confusing, contradictory, or erroneous. Luke seems to regard the reader's prior instruction and information as insufficient or misleading. If the reader is in reality a Roman official who may, in the near future, have to make decisions concerning these Christians, getting the story straight is of extreme importance. If the reader is a recently catechized Christian, having the story in order would be fruitful for clarity of identity, defense against heresy, certainty in witnessing, and maturity of faith. As the Deuteronomic historian did for Israel by reflecting upon his history and interpreting documents of that history, so Luke sets himself to do for the Christian community.

The word "interpreting" is crucial here. There is no evidence that Luke regards the many narratives already in existence as "only interpretations" that he will counter with a purely objective account of only the facts. Notice that his research is in the traditional accounts of eyewitnesses and ministers of the Word. This means the story is already in the form of Christian interpretation and proclamation. The term "eyewitness" does not refer to neutral observers (Luke 24:48). The role of being a witness cannot be filled by someone who is physically present but who does not believe. Luke is clear on this point: Jesus' way of life *all* could know; Jesus' death by crucifixion *all* could know; that God raised him from the dead, of that *we* are witnesses (Acts 2:22-32). Therefore, Luke's reader can expect from him a narrative that not only tells what was apparently happening, but what was *really* happening as faith understood what God was doing in and through persons and events. Luke lets the reader see what no camera will pick up and hear what no recorder will receive. Expressions as verifiable as "In the fifteenth year of the reign of Tiberius Caesar" and as confessional as "and the Holy Spirit said" make equal claim upon the attention of the reader. We are not getting from Luke two stories—the historian's and the believer's—but one. How much of it was already in this form when it came to Luke we do not know, but as it is now narrated, this one continuous story is the author's witness. It is the fruit of close research, now presented as an orderly account, so that the reader, already having been informed, may now have certainty.

● The form of Luke's writing, an orderly account of the ministry of Jesus, set within the larger story of Israel before him and of the church after him, is a deliberately chosen literary vehicle. In 1:1-4 he wants that to be understood. He implies that *how* he has shaped the material is integral to *what* he seeks to achieve. It is imperative that the modern interpreter recognize what this evangelist intends and how that affects his total presentation.

A historical presentation such as Luke's presumes that quite a bit of time has passed since the events narrated took place. This has a positive side in that there can now be reflection on the sequence, the continuity, and the overall significance of events of the past. One can now see the right and wrong of things, the key moments' significance, missed in the moments themselves, and how God's will was at work even in dark and threatening deeds. The negative side is that the passing of time often means a loss of enthusiasm, of commitment, of memory, and of leadership by death and distance. It may also mean a loss of unity as the story is fragmented into stories that favor particular persons and places and viewpoints, and thus a loss of identity as well. Because the passing of time has such positive values and yet poses such dangers, a history has to be written.

Luke's presentation of the story as history also presumes that much more time will pass before the end. One does not research and write an orderly account if one is motivated by the conviction that the Day of the Lord is at hand. If some early Christians were pilgrims gazing into heaven, eventually they would need help in adjusting to a new posture with a minimal loss of faith and hope. Without that help, despair and cynicism, with the behavior that accompanies those attitudes, could take over and destroy the community. In that time of the church's need there were varied reactions to the delay. Some made slight adjustments in their calendars and repeated the old announcements of the end. Others denied the future, claiming that the experiences of the present moment ended all search for meaning in the horizons of past and future. Luke responded by gathering the scattered words and events that had taken place, framing them into an orderly account, and setting that account of Jesus Christ in the center of history.

● It is extremely important that the interpreter deal with Luke 1:1-4, especially if there are to be several lessons or sermons from this Gospel. While seeming not to be as exciting as other passages, these verses can hardly be surpassed for significant instruction and clarification. Here one finds insight into the growth of the Christian tradition, the development of interpretation, and the making of a book of the New Testament. Here also one is disabused of magical views of inspiration; Luke did research, questioned, and made judgments about his sources. In addition, Luke's description of his purpose is a reminder that one vital dynamic in all teaching and preaching is that of enabling listeners to know "the truth concerning the things of which you have been informed" (v 4). All of us need help understanding what we already know. Luke-Acts is not offered as new information but as a new perspective on the familiar. That often is a word of judgment and of liberation.

Finally, Luke is instructive in his presentation of the Christian life as participation in the larger and longer story of what God is doing in the church and in the world. To those who tend to evacuate the present in longing for some golden age of the past, Luke-Acts is a reminder that each time and place is God's time and place, here and now no less than there and then. And for those who reduce the entire Christian faith to private experiences of the heart, there is no better corrective than the narrative before us.

Luke 4:16-30
The Rejection at Nazareth

Luke 4:16-30 is a distinct unit, describing an event geographically separate from what precedes and what follows. It suffers no violation when investigated apart from the context, although, as we shall see, the particular location of this story in Luke forces certain questions to the surface.

● The interpreter may need to call attention to the violation of this text by lectionaries and commentaries that divide the passage at v 21. By closing the reading at that point modern listeners are able to join the congregation at Nazareth in bragging about Jesus ("they all spoke well of him," v 22). But being complimentary of the preacher after the reading of the text (vv 17-21), but before the sermon, proved to be premature. It is Jesus' sermon (vv 23-30) and the congregation's response that Luke wants us to hear. And this is what we need to hear, not only as interpreters of Luke, but as disciples of this Jesus who so disturbs his audience.

This passage serves as an excellent place to remind ourselves just how profoundly teaching and preaching are affected by observing or not observing the natural boundaries of a text.

First, however, it is important to clear the mind of Jesus' rejection in Nazareth as told by Mark and Matthew.

The church's memory of Jesus' return to his home synagogue is that of a man's return to the scenes of childhood and youth and the discovery that familiarity blinds the local citizens to who he is and what he is doing. Relatives and friends are both astonished and offended, in response to which Jesus cites the old proverb about a prophet having no honor in his own country. This memory is based on Mark's brief account (6:1-6), which Matthew followed rather closely (13:54-58). If this recollection is brought to Luke 4, it will distort one's understanding of the more elaborate, more complex, and more theologically intentional account in this Gospel. Even though Luke obviously has in mind the same event that Mark narrates, and even though there are a few lines in the two accounts that are very similar, one has to conclude that Luke here draws upon a separate tradition. Whatever may have been the form of the story in Luke's source, as it now stands it provides a preview of Luke's understanding of the mission of Jesus.

The location of this story in the Gospel is itself an important clue to Luke's reason for using it. Unlike Mark and Matthew,

Luke places the return to Nazareth at the opening of Jesus' ministry. After Jesus' baptism and temptation, he returned in the power of the Spirit to Galilee, and this story is told following a general statement about Jesus' travels, synagogue teaching, and public acclaim. Chronologically this location is impossible. The story assumes Jesus has been away from Nazareth for some time, perhaps living elsewhere (Capernaum?), and it assumes that Jesus has already performed mighty works in Capernaum, reports of which have come to Nazareth. Actually, it is not until the next paragraph (4:31-37) that Jesus goes to Capernaum and performs miracles. Why would Luke render his chronology senseless? Obviously, something is more important than correct chronology, and Luke's "orderly account" of events is to be unfolded according to a principle more vital than historical sequence. He had sacrificed chronology earlier by telling of the imprisonment of John the Baptist *before* he told of Jesus' baptism 3:19-22). Whatever the price he has to pay, Luke definitely wants this story here. Why?

It is possible that Luke places the story of Jesus' rejection in Nazareth here in order to continue a theme developed in the preceding stories. Thus, Jesus receives the Holy Spirit at his baptism (3:22); Jesus, full of the Holy Spirit, goes from the Jordan and is led by the Spirit for forty days in the wildnerness, and tempted by the devil (4:1-2): Jesus in the power of the Spirit returns to Galilee (4:14); and now in the synagogue at Nazareth, he reads from Isaiah, "The Spirit of the Lord is upon me . . ." (4:18). Jesus' ministry is led, empowered, and anointed by the Holy Spirit. By the power of the Spirit Jesus had rejected the tempter's offer of false forms of ministry, and now in the full confidence of that Spirit he launches the ministry for which God has anointed him.

With the word "launch," we have already introduced the principal reason for placing this story at the beginning of Jesus' ministry. It is a programmatic story, previewing all that is to follow and summarizing Luke's understanding of what God is doing in Jesus of Nazareth. Perhaps a brief sketch of the main themes will aid our grasp of 4:16-30 and provide a clearer overview of the whole of Luke's message.

● The remainder of this discussion of Luke 4:16-30 will depart from the pattern used for previous texts. Instead of an exploration of the passage, followed by comments suggesting interpretations for the present, in what follows, past and present are woven into one discussion. This procedure seems appropriate, not only to Luke's narrative style, but also to his theology, which understands what God was doing and is doing as one continuous story. Interpreting Luke, therefore, not only permits but demands the extension of the commentary into our own times. In addition, this text offers an opportunity to illustrate a point discussed as Procedural Guideline 5, p. 22. The interpreter should consider, if possible, adopting the form of the text as the form for the lesson or sermon. Luke invites and challenges us to interpret narratively.

1. The ministry of Jesus Christ and of his church began in the bosom of Judaism. In Nazareth where he was brought up in Judaism (recall Luke's stories of Jesus' circumcision, dedication, visit to the temple at age twelve), in the synagogue where Jesus worshiped "as his custom was," through the reading of the prophet Isaiah, in a sermon about Elijah and Elisha, Jesus launched his mission. He was not an outsider or a rebel but one of Israel's own, and his ministry never lost its embrace of that heritage. Likewise, the early church continued in synagogue and temple. Even Paul, missionary to the nations, always went first to the synagogue, says Luke. Jesus and the church are carrying out what God had intended all along.

2. God has not rejected Israel to embrace the church, but Israel has rejected her own purpose and mission. Luke wants it to be clearly understood that the fundamental quarrel is not

between the synagogue and the church but between the synagogue and its own Scriptures. Jesus addressed an Israel under the judgment of her own past, her own prophets, her own authoritative texts. Extending the ministry of God's care to human needs beyond the bounds of Israel is not a new development; it has been native to Israel since the time of Isaiah, Elijah, and Elisha. The church, as the new Israel, should listen carefully; for her history likewise documents her failure to listen to her own Scriptures. Scripture functions, not only as a support for the life and work of the church, but also as the standard of value by which that life and work are judged. When this critical function of Scripture is ignored or denied, then the people of God are tempted to "use" Scripture to bless values and prejudices purchased wholesale from the merchants of culture.

3. Proximity to and familiarity with the persons, events, places, and texts of religion can easily be a privilege that blinds. The scene in Nazareth is only one of many occasions on which Luke stresses this point. Distant Nineveh will judge this place because Nineveh repented when Jonah preached, and one greater than Jonah is in your midst. The queen of the South traveled from another continent to her Solomon, and here among you is one greater than Solomon (11:29-32). Of course, in the judgment, says Luke, you will claim your privileges as free passes, recalling times when you had dinner with Jesus or when he preached in your town (13:26-27), but to no avail. It will not even count in the Kingdom to claim to be a relative of Jesus. When a woman in Jesus' audience blessed Jesus' mother, Luke tells us Jesus countered that the blessing belongs only to those who hear and keep God's word (11:27-28). The church should still be listening, for if God's true Israel is continued in the church, we can be quite sure that the privilege continues to be just as perilous. The pattern of Jesus' ministry that Luke

describes—going to his own people, being rejected, taking the message to others—was repeated in Paul's ministry and, unless the warning is heard, can be repeated in our time.

4. Jesus of Nazareth is the promised Servant of God who is anointed ("anointed one" = Christ) by the Holy Spirit to inaugurate the Kingdom, turning hope to reality and translating ancient texts into proclamations of the New Age. That which is announced is amnesty, liberation, and the restored joys of the Year of Jubilee (vv 18-19).[17] The time of the beginning of the "acceptable year of the Lord" is now. "Today this scripture has been fulfilled in your hearing" (v 21). Luke uses "today" in this sense eleven times (more than Mark or Matthew), pointing to his view of the ministry of Jesus as fulfillment of the expected last days. The sign of the end time is the outpouring of the Holy Spirit (Joel 2:27-32; Acts 2:17-18), which is the hallmark of Jesus' ministry. However, after Jesus' ascension, the Holy Spirit is poured out upon the church (24:49; Acts 1:4-5), signifying that the church, too, is living in the end time. For Luke, therefore, the time of Jesus is the last days, but not the *very* last. If, therefore, the church participates with Jesus in the fulfillment of the end time and in its sign—the power of the Holy Spirit—the "today" of Luke 4 is still the "today" of the church. Whatever else this means, it certainly says that ancient texts with their promises of "someday" for the poor, the imprisoned, and the dispossessed are no longer promises but proclamations and mandates. "Today this scripture has been fulfilled."

5. Anger and murder are the last defenses of even the religious who sense their identity and way of life being threatened. And when the threat consists of painful reminders of what is already known, but not embraced, the anger is

[17]For a description of the Year of Jubilee, see Lev. 25:8-12.

intensified. Solving problems by making casualties of those who remind us of our contradictions is as old as Cain, as new as the morning paper. The worshipers at Nazareth know that God had blessed a Syro-Phoenician through Elijah's ministry, and they know that God had cured a Syrian through Elisha. But it was more than they wanted to know, and they certainly did not appreciate being reminded (vv 25-28). Wherever lines of race, custom, and nationality are religiously guarded, the announcement that God responds to human needs "regardless" is hardly good news. Solution: stone Jesus by dashing him against the rocks in a deep ravine (v 29). The attempt was unsuccessful (v 30), but if one moves the scene not many miles and not many months, another crowd with the same motivation will succeed.

Like Elijah, the prophet Jesus was a troubler in Israel. Israel's problem, says Luke, was ignorance ("Father, forgive them; for they know not what they do," 23:34; "And now, brethren, I know that you acted in ignorance, as did also your rulers," Acts 3:17), but it was not an ignorance to be relieved by more books, more study. There is a kind of ignorance that calls for repentance.

Luke 15:11-32
The Parable of the Loving Father

This familiar parable is a good example of the literary quality of Luke's whole Gospel. Moreover, its characters have a universal appeal, and it portrays the common human struggle with forgiveness, which fulfills our sense of what is right, yet violates it at the same time. The claim of this text upon our attention at the present is due to its being so characteristically Lukan in both form and content. In form, it has the excellent literary style of which we have spoken, and it is a parable, again characteristic of Luke. Apart from the birth and infancy stories, the major body of material in Luke that is not in Mark or

Matthew consists of parables. In content, this passage carries the central affirmation of Luke's theology: the paradox of an offer of the *unconditional* grace of a God who is kind to the ungrateful and selfish, coupled with a demand for repentance as the *condition* for forgiveness of sins.

Some things have already been said about parables in the course of discussing Matthew 25:1-13. But that discussion was primarily intended as preparation for a Matthean parable, and Matthew's parables hardly prepare us for those in Luke. While the two Gospels have some parables in common, as well as some derived from Mark, Luke's own parables are more like human interest stories and have more complex characterizations. Except in his nature parables, Matthew depends heavily on the master/servant relationship as his basic analogy. Luke, however, focuses on other dimensions of the human community: a father and his sons, a widow and a judge, a rich man and a beggar, a tax collector and a Pharisee, a friend seeking to borrow bread at midnight.

● A major task in the interpretation of parables is to make sure that the parable itself is not lost in the process of its interpretation.[18] On the one hand, the parable can be lost by being transformed into an allegory, a form of spiritualizing of a story in which it is understood to be saying something other than what it is saying. Allegorical interpretation of parables began quite early, as the New Testament itself testifies (Mark 4:13-20; Matt 13:36-43). On the other hand, the parable can be lost by being distilled into a single thesis or proposition, a violation comparable to giving children the themes or points to bedtime stories as a substitute for the stories themselves. To lose the art of the story itself is sometimes called the "heresy of paraphrase." It is to forget that a parable as parable, not only says something, but does something. Of course, the interpreter will need to explore terms and phrases in order to hear the story for what it says.

[18]Perrin, *Jesus and the Language of the Kingdom,* pp. 89-168.

Commentaries must be consulted for the interpreter to understand, for example, the inheritance laws of Jesus' time, the rights
of younger and older brothers, and the significance of robes and
rings. But all this is done to give both interpreter and audience the
ears of the first hearers so that the parable will again be fresh and
new. The interpreter may discover in the process that even after
dozens of references to and uses of this parable, it is now heard for
the first time.

Luke 15:11-32 is a single unit, contrary to the opinion of some
who regard vv 25-32 as an expansion of the original story. That
the father's dealings with the two sons constitute one story is
persuasively argued by the context (esp. 15:1-2), and by the
formal features of the two episodes that are parallel in many
ways. And both episodes close with essentially the same
statement by the father (vv 24, 32). One may see the unity of the
story by keeping in mind the opening line: "There was a man
who had two sons." This is a parable of a father with two sons,
not a parable of a son who had a father and a brother.

This parable is the third in a trilogy given by Luke in response
to the Pharisees' and scribes' criticism lodged against Jesus'
practice of table fellowship with sinners. Although the three
parables have a common theme (concern for the lost), they are
in fact quite different, and it is possible that only the third was
originally given as a response to the criticism that Jesus ate with
sinners. Luke has collected these parables under an umbrella
theme, just as Mark 4 and Matthew 13 are collections by those
writers. The parable of the sheep concerns seeking the lost,
with an accent on the risk and cost (leaving ninety-nine *in the
wilderness* and not safely in a fold), and finally on the joy of
finding the lost sheep. The parable of the coin concerns seeking
the lost, with an accent on diligent expenditure of time and
effort on what seems to some to be of little value, and finally the
joy of finding. The parable of the father has the note of

rejoicing, but there is no search for the lost. The first two parables have a closing comment about joy over a sinner who repents, even though the sheep and the coin hardly depict repentance unless, of course, being found is a form of (or a prelude to) repentance. On the other hand, the third parable does involve repentance, but has no closing comment about it. The conclusion must be drawn by the hearer. Such is the function of a parable, to precipitate judgment and action by the listeners. If this parable was addressed to Pharisees and scribes, then whether or not the older son went in to the party was for them to decide. For Luke to tell this parable without a closing comment or judgment in relation to the critics of Jesus, may indicate that in Luke's time and place the mission to the Jews was still open. That is to say, the church was still at work in the Jewish community, with at least some doors still open for conversation.

● The interpreter will want to avoid two popular ways of handling the story. The one is to engage heavily in psychological speculations about conditions of home life, what the unmentioned mother was like, sibling rivalries, favorite son syndromes, and listening to wild geese. All that may be true, but no one knows that it is, and the parable is not telling. The other is to cartoon the two sons, the younger as the fun-loving, gregarious life-of-the-party whom everybody loves, the older as a penny-pinching, sour-spirited grouch who has never laughed and in whose presence no one else can. The fact is, the father had two sons. One had no claim because he alienated himself from family and faith, sinking to the level of an apostate. The other felt he had a claim on his father on the grounds of faithfulness, hard work, and complete obedience. "Which son do you like the best?" is hardly the issue here.

Just as table fellowship prompted the parable, so is the party the crux of the matter. That party is the surprise of abundant grace and the offense to calculated righteousness. That party throws out of joint every line of traditional wisdom about moral upbringing and reaping what you sow. Every religion worth its salt has rites and processes for the restoration of the erring, but they are rites of sackcloth and ashes, nor rings and robes, of bread and water, not fatted calf, of silence and prayer, not music and dancing. A party? Many of us have enjoyed it from afar and scolded the pouting older brother, but who among us would have gone to that party? Does not the party give the impression of condoning, of blessing or rewarding the prodigal? Is there anything in the banquet, the laughter, the dancing, and the music that gives moral and doctrinal instruction, that warns of waste and denial of faith, that builds a fence against future repeats of squandered life? The moral and ethical undergirding of a stable society suffers attack by that party. The questions raised by the older son are not simply the jealous barbs of a greedy dullard. By all the standards that preserve hearth and home, church and society, he makes sense. To portray him otherwise would not only be unrealistic, but would rob the parable of power. The issue is profound, extremely difficult, and always with us. Everyone applauds forgiving love. However, the fact remains that it is also in constant danger of becoming a cheap blessing, erosive to all ethical seriousness.

• It is not uncommon for the preacher or teacher of this parable to be so concerned to aim the story at younger son types or older son types that in the service of the exhortation, the teacher may present one son favorably and one unfavorably. In other words, one becomes the dark background to enhance the portrait of the other. To do this is to treat the parable as an "either/or" story, giving the impression that one type of behavior is accepted and the other rejected. This is not an "either/or" story but a "both/and" story. The father is not choosing between his sons; he goes out to both, he affirms his love for both. Table fellowship with sinners is no rejection of Pharisees. Perhaps the offense of the Gospel lies just here: God is a "both/and" God, embracing both Jew and Greek, both bond and free, both male and female, both saint and sinner. Those of us with "either/or" biases are offended by a God who is so impartial as to send sun and rain on the good and evil alike. Jonah expressed it well, in angry defense of his refusal to preach in Nineveh: "I made haste to flee to Tarshish; for I knew that thou art a gracious god and merciful, slow to anger and abounding in steadfast love" (Jon 4:2).

Luke 24:13-35
On the Road to Emmaus

This story is set between the account of the apostles' initial unbelief upon hearing the report from the women at the empty tomb and the account of Christ's appearance to them, which created among the apostles joyous disbelief and wonder (24:41). The appearance to the two disciples on the road to Emmaus therefore functions as a bridge story between definite disbelief ("these words seemed to them an idle tale") and cautious belief.

This narrative has no parallel in the Gospels. Those students of the Gospel who have regarded the resurrection appearances as narrative elaborations of the very early Gospel traditions preserved in First Corinthians 15:5-8 ("he appeared to Cephas, then to the twelve. Then he appeared to more than five hundred brethren at one time, most of whom are still alive, though some have fallen asleep. Then he appeared to James, then to all the apostles. Last of all, as to one untimely born, he appeared also to me"), must recognize this story as not fitting the pattern. Cleopas and the other disciple are not mentioned in that tradition. In fact, apart from this story they are unknown, unless they are the same Clopas and his wife Mary mentioned in John 19:25. However, Mary was at the tomb, and Cleopas' companion (man or woman?) was not (24:22).

We do not know in what form this narrative came to Luke. Two items in it argue for Palestinian origin and perhaps an early date. First, this account contains the only reference in the Gospels to the appearance to Simon Peter (24:34), otherwise referred to only in the early tradition (1 Cor 15:5).[19] Second, in this story, Jesus is presented in the context of messianic expectations in Israel (24:19-21) and not in the categories of the Christologies that prevailed in the Gentile churches as we know them through Paul. This second characteristic of the account could, however, be Luke's contribution to the narrative, since the continuity of Jesus' mission and passion with Israel's own hopes is a consistent theme in Luke-Acts.

In fact, whatever its source and earlier shape, the account of Jesus' appearance on the way to Emmaus is definitely a Lukan story. It is clearly a self-contained narrative, having its own geographical and chronological frame, its own introduction and conclusion, and all the formal features of a well-constructed story. There are names and places, there is anticipation moving to a climax, and a wide range of human motions are evoked. This resurrection appearance is told to us in the style of an accomplished storyteller. Hermann Gunkel, the famous Old Testament scholar of another generation, once compared this story to the oldest Genesis stories of God's appearances incognito (e.g., the appearance of the Lord to Abraham at Mamre, described as the sudden presence of three visitors—Gen 18:1-15).

But if Luke the storyteller gives us pleasure, which he does, Luke the theologian reminds us that his literary skills are in the service of the Gospel, which is presented so that a reader having been informed of these things may now understand that

[19]Mark 16:7 may imply an appearance to Peter; also a few ancient manuscripts add after Luke 24:11 a line about Peter's coming to the tomb. This is obviously a borrowing from John 20:1-10.

information. Therefore just as earlier he had woven into the beautiful song of Mary revolutionary lines of social, political, and economic reversals (1:46-55), so here in this moving story he presses home two themes central to his theology. At the risk of inflicting the kind of harm that analysis may do to a story, let us isolate those two themes for special attention. One, the mission, and especially the passion, of Christ is a central message of the Old Testament. The other, table fellowship, is of profound importance as the occasion for experiencing the presence of Christ. To express Luke's themes in modern church language, Luke 24:13-35 is a story of the Gospel as word and sacrament.

● We have already spoken of the importance of the Old Testament for Luke's narrative of Christ and the church. The interpreter can hardly overemphasize this fact, especially in view of the popular sloganized error: "Matthew was written for Jews, Luke for Gentiles." Over and over, from birth stories to resurrection appearances, from Bethlehem to Rome, Luke tells his readers that Jesus and the church are the fulfillment of, not a digression from, Israel's hope and mission in the world. Jesus and the church lived according to the Scriptures, but suffered at the hands of Israel because she did not understand her own Scriptures. In continuity with Israel, says Luke, Jerusalem was the center of the church's life and mission, the temple and the synagogue were revered institutions, and "the Twelve" were the foundation of the believing community.[20] With this in mind, look at the text before us.

The risen Christ joins two dejected disciples, "And beginning with Moses and all the prophets, he interpreted to them in all the scriptures the things concerning himself" (v 27). The disciples do not know who Jesus is, however. To

[20]Acts 1:12-26 reveals how important it is for Luke that the Twelve, reduced to eleven by Judas' act, become again Twelve.

them he is a stranger, as he was to Israel. Just as at the transfiguration and ascension, "clouds" and "sleep" preserve the revealed/concealed quality of God's revelation in Christ (Luke 9:28-31; Acts 1:6-11), so here Luke says, "But their eyes were kept from recognizing him" (v 16). Why? Because faith is not generated by an experience of being overwhelmed but by gaining clarity about the true meaning of scripture. As the two disciples reflected on the experience they said, "Did not our hearts burn within us while he talked to us on the road, *while he opened to us the scriptures?*" (v 32). For Luke, the way of God in the world is plain: "If they do not hear Moses and the prophets, neither will they be convinced if someone should rise from the dead" (16:31).

The knowledge of scripture is made possible with the resurrection. It comes as no surprise, therefore, to find that Luke's other appearance narrative is a parallel to the Emmaus story. Christ appeared in Jerusalem to the eleven and those with them. "Then he said to them, 'These are my words which I spoke to you, while I was still with you, that everything written about me in the law of Moses and the prophets and the psalms must be fulfilled.' Then he opened their minds to understand the scriptures" (24:44-45). From Jesus to the disciples after resurrection, from the disciples to synagogue and temple audiences after the outpouring of the Holy Spirit (Acts 2:1ff.), the correct interpretation of scripture was given. This new understanding is the substance of the preaching of the church in Acts. This understanding of scripture now breaks the hold of ignorance over the mind and enables the one who believes to see that the word through Israel, through Christ, and through the church is one and the same: it is the purpose of God to bless all nations of the world.

If the church has continuity with Christ and Judaism through the correct understanding of scripture, it has the experience of immediacy in that relationship through the sacrament of table fellowship. The word "sacrament" seems appropriate since Luke presents the meal in Emmaus as the Eucharist: "When he was at table with them, he took the bread and blessed, and broke it, and gave it to them" (v 30). It was apparently in this act that their eyes were opened and they recognized Jesus. As the two told it later in Jerusalem, "He was known to them in the breaking of the bread" (v 35). After the ascension of Christ, the church has continued to experience the presence during the absence, and that experience occurs, not exclusively, but certainly, in table fellowship.

It is important for the church, in her fervent desire to capture the Emmaus moment in her continuing life, to remember that the two disciples at Emmaus did not prepare a sacrament and hope Christ would be present. They were hospitable to a weary stranger, offering to share their bread. This is the Lukan touch not to be missed. Had they known before the invitation that the stranger was Christ, one can imagine the red carpet and elaborate preparations. But it was with a tired and hungry traveler that they shared bread. They prepared supper, and his presence made it a sacrament. The story could be read as a narrative unfolding of Matthew's "I was a stranger . . . as you did it to one of the least of these my brethren, you did it to me" (25:35-40).

• This text could well provide an occasion for the interpreter to recall or to review in Luke the frequency and significance of table fellowship. Some of the great lessons and moving stories were shared when Jesus was at table. It would be helpful to the interpreter to move through the entire Gospel noting these, just to sense the cumulative effect of their number and variety. At table Jesus spoke of life in the Kingdom—in the home of Martha and Mary, as the guest of Simon the Pharisee, while observing hosts and guests at a banquet, in response to attacks because he ate with sinners, and many others. And in The Acts of the Apostles table fellowship continued as a significant act of the church's life. In fact, Acts opens with a scene of the risen Christ eating with ("staying" in the RSV is a translation of the word meaning "sharing the salt") the apostles (1:4). At table is not a casual time, a recess from Kingdom business; rather, it *is* the Kingdom.

This attention to table fellowship seemingly occurs at different levels, but in reality it is one level. Luke may be stressing simply the importance of sharing food. The poor are to be cared for; the church is to give attention to breaking bread to relieve hunger. Such was the program of sharing in the church at Jerusalem. Luke's story of the rich man and Lazarus is a story of torment and paradise, the difference resting entirely on one fact: one man ate and one did not. Where that occurs you do not have the Kingdom. And for Luke, breaking bread to meet hunger and breaking bread as a sacrament are not two different levels of spirituality; they are the same meal if Christ is present. Furthermore, just as table fellowship was clear evidence of the full acceptance of sinners by Jesus, so table fellowship was the sign of full accord in the church. Recall Simon Peter's housetop vision that called him to go preach to Gentiles at Caesarea (Acts 10). The vision was a vision of food, both Jewish and non-Jewish, and the vision was fulfilled in Peter's eating with Gentiles. When called on the carpet in Jerusalem, Peter had to respond to the charge, not that he had preached to or baptized non-Jews, but that he had eaten with them (Acts 11:3). That, says Luke, is the crux of the matter. The church has no right to try to evangelize people with whom it will not eat. The passing of the centuries has hardly rendered that principle void, or irrelevant.

After examining Luke 24:13-35 to ascertain Luke's themes and intent, the interpreter has to deal with the question of the most appropriate form for communicating the material. Again, why not try to follow Luke? He has beautifully demonstrated that profound theological content can be communicated in a narrative. His two volumes offer many vivid examples, but none more compelling than this story of the appearance of the risen Christ on the way to Emmaus.

THE GOSPEL OF JOHN

If Matthew has been the Gospel most used in the church's doctrine and liturgy, John has been the Gospel most loved by the church's membership.[21] It is the source of many favorite phrases, images, and teachings of the Christian community: "For God so loved the world," "Let not your hearts be troubled," "I am the resurrection and the life," "A new commandment I give to you," "By this shall all men know that you are my disciples," "In the beginning was the Word," "I pray, Father, that they may be one," "And the Word became flesh and dwelt among us," and on and on.

● The interpreter will find this "favorite" status an advantage in that the appetite to explore and understand this Gospel is already present and a strong motivator. On the other hand, this same fact of John's Gospel being a favorite Gospel will function as a disadvantage because honest study often bears fruit quite different from popular and sometimes sentimental appropriations of a text. Arriving at new understandings of a favorite book can be an experience similar to watching a favorite landscape being

[21]Check the commentaries for the debate about authorship. John the apostle is not mentioned by name in this Gospel. Insertion of the name by *The Living Bible* has no support in the text.

bulldozed in order to build low-cost housing for the poor. Discoveries are not always welcome, and the head may have to work overtime to find reasons that will adequately ease the pain in a reluctant heart.

Very likely the church that finds the person and the promises of Jesus Christ more immediate and available in this Gospel than in any other would be surprised to hear scholars speak of standing before John as before a locked door, fumbling for the right key. In fact, the church would probably be shocked to learn that his Gospel has from earliest times created sharp disagreements among interpreters, some claiming that the portrait of Christ presented by John is dangerously close to that heretical view that argued that the divine Son did not really become human but only seemed to do so. It is quite possible that the vigorous doctrinal dispute reflected in the Epistles of John arose out of different understandings of this Gospel. We do know that in the early centuries of the church there was strong suspicion of the Gospel of John in orthodox circles. The central issue was whether or not the Christ of this Gospel stands in too little continuity with the historical Jesus. That remains a central issue and one which will arise in our discussion here. But throughout the process of teaching and preaching John's Gospel, the interpreter should remain sensitive to the church's embrace of and difficulties with this exciting and venturesome retelling of the Gospel of Jesus Christ. Over and over again the careful reader will be reminded of the truth of the oft-quoted statement: "This is a book in which a child can wade and an elephant can swim."

Regardless of one's sense of familiarity with this Gospel, reading through it again remains the best first step in interpretation. An important benefit of this reading is the creation of the distance from the Synoptics necessary for listening to John's unique statement of the gospel. This distance will be appropriate, because it will not be due to a theory about John in relation to the other Gospels, but will be derived from the text itself. This distance will also be honest, without that exaggeration common to some interpreters who do not acknowledge the considerable amount of subject matter this Gospel has in common with one or more of the Synoptics. In common, though differently handled, are accounts of John the Baptist, Jesus going into Galilee, feeding the multitudes, walking on water, the miraculous catch of fish, Peter's confession, Martha and Mary, Jesus' entry into Jerusalem, a last supper with his disciples, etc.

But beyond question, the strongest impression is that of difference from the other Gospels. Noticeably absent are acts of exorcism, parables, ethical instructions like those found in the Sermon on the Mount, messianic secrecy, and Jesus' struggles in the wilderness of temptation and in Gethsemane. Noticeably present are new stories: the wedding at Cana, Nicodemus coming to Jesus at night, the woman at the well, the healing at the pool, the raising of Lazarus. Perhaps less noticeable, but very significant, are the different arrangements of materials (e.g., the cleansing of the temple comes near the beginning rather than near the end), John the Baptist and Jesus have concurrent ministries, rather than Jesus' beginning after John is in prison; and the impression of a longer ministry for Jesus, perhaps three or more years rather than one, if calculated by the number of visits he made to Jerusalem.

Most striking to the reader is the radically different portrait of Jesus Christ. He is a historical figure in John, to be sure, located in time and place, having family and friends, eating and drinking, getting weary and thirsty, bleeding and dying. But these descriptions recede behind the stronger image of Jesus being from above, eternally at home with God whom he reveals in word and sign. "He who has seen me has seen the Father" (14:9). Because he knows that he has come from God and goes again to God (13:3), the Johannine Christ has no need for anyone to tell him anything (2:25). He ministers according to divine plan ("my hour") and not according to the instructions or advice or requests of others (2:1-4; 7:1-10; 11:1-7). His prayers are sermonic for the benefit of those nearby (11:42), and when the hour of death comes, he remains in control. He has the power to lay down his life and the power to take it up again (10:17-18).

Quite understandably, most of his listeners have difficulty with the words of this one from heaven. He speaks of the temple, and his audience thinks of wood and stone (2:19-21); he speaks of a new birth, and Nicodemus thinks of his mother's womb (3:3-4); he speaks of water of life, and the Samaritan woman thinks of well and bucket (4:10-11); he speaks of the food that sustains, and his disciples wonder who brought his lunch (4:31-33). But his words and his deeds are not altogether mysterious; there is a faith, an insight, a knowledge born of willingness to do God's will (7:17), which can hear the Word in the words and see the truth beyond the signs.

● Interpreters of John need to be on guard against slipping into that kind of theological arrogance that unfairly judges those who do not see what they see. The writer of this Gospel is offering the witness of a community that was able to affirm, "We have beheld his glory" (1:14), and he writes to generate the faith that sees as that community does (20:31). What may be forgotten by the interpreter is that the faith of the early Christians was born of a "because of/in spite of" encounter with Christ. God was not only revealed, but also concealed, in Jesus of Nazareth. That "we" have beheld his glory and bear witness to what was seen and heard does not mean that all saw and heard. We are not dealing here with words and deeds that had "God" written all over them. Faith was not then, nor is it now, exempted from risk and decision.

Once faith is generated and one is able to see and hear the revelation of God, the natural inclination is to take what was heard in a whisper and shout it from the housetop. That is as it should be, but the one who shouts must beware lest he criticize and judge too quickly those who do not hear for not being able to grasp what seems so absolutely clear to the believer. The interpreter would do well to remember that those who first saw and heard Jesus did not have a copy of the prologue to John (1:1-18) to give them immediately the eyes and ears of faith.

This entire Gospel seems to be structured so as to present Jesus as the Revealer of God. "No one has ever seen God; the only Son, who is in the bosom of the Father, he has made him known" (1:18). Every story, every sign, and every discourse makes this point. The following broad outline might help to make the permeating and controlling nature of this theme visible:

Prologue	1:1-18
The Revealer of God ministers on earth	1:19–12:50
The Revealer of God returns to glory	13:1–20:31
Epilogue	21:1-25

Within this outline there are basically three kinds of material. First, there are the "revelation discourses," lengthy speeches that focus upon the meaning and nature of true and eternal life. This life is described as knowing God as he is revealed and offered through his Son, Jesus Christ (17:3). Then there are the "signs," the seven revelatory acts (eight if chap. 21 is included), which usually prompt the revelatory discourses. These signs are:

Turning water to wine (2:1-11)
Healing a nobleman's son (4:46-54)
Healing the lame man at the pool (5:2-9)
Feeding the multitude (6:1-15)

Walking on water (6:16-21)
Healing the blind man (9:1-7)
Raising Lazarus (11:1-44)
Providing a large catch of fish (21:1-14)

The third type of material is the passion narrative, which may have come to the writer as a complete unit, even though it, too, is Johannine in its present form. This was very likely the part of the tradition that was least modified in being told and retold. It was and is the inner sanctum of all the Gospels.

Some scholars are persuaded it is possible to discern stages in the development of this Gospel prior to its present form. One may consult the more recent commentaries for the evidence and the counter arguments. The task before us here is to investigate texts representative of the three commonly accepted kinds of material in John: the revelation discourses, the signs, and the passion narrative. These three will be prefaced by an exploration of the Prologue. In this way, some of the major themes of Johannine theology can be introduced: God's relation to the world, miracles as signs, eternal life, the Holy Spirit, and the significance of the death of Jesus.

Before we move to these representative texts, a word should be said about the purposes of this Gospel. On the face of it, the writer himself has answered our question: "But these are written that you may believe that Jesus is the Christ, the Son of God, and that believing you may have life in his name" (20:31). That would appear to define the Gospel as a missionary or evangelistic document, designed to generate faith. But generate whose faith? Certainly not the Jews'; in John they are portrayed as the epitome of what it means to be "of the world," and one would hardly expect converts from such a group. The writer seems to be building his case *against* the synagogue, not seeking to make inroads into it.

The synagogue faction is not the only group against which this Gospel develops a polemic. Great pains are taken to make sure everyone understands that John the Baptist was not the Christ, but that he was, rather, subordinate to the Christ. The Baptist's sole function was to witness to the Christ (1:5-8, 15; 1:19-42; 3:25-30; 5:33-36). Being only a witness, says the Gospel, John gladly released his own disciples to join Jesus. It would seem that the Fourth Gospel was written when and where the sect of John the Baptist was of such size and vitality as to call for a response by the Christian community. But since John the Baptist disappears after chapter 5, it hardly seems reasonable to assume the author's stated evangelistic purpose was aimed primarily at this group.

A real possibility is that the author's concern was not to win new converts, but to confirm the faith of his own community and to correct the faith of those whose beliefs he regarded as erroneous. That this Gospel assumes its readers are Christian seems clear. For example, the farewell speeches and prayer (chaps. 14–17) are "within the community" materials. But the stress upon the *truth* and what is *true* implies that some members within this or a nearby Christian community need the discipline of the right word. This Gospel seems to be directed not to persons who need to hear the Word for the first time, but to those who need to hear the *true* Word.[22]

John 1:1-18
The Prologue

● The interpreter of the Gospel of John will experience at least two temptations. The first will be the temptation to pass over the prologue, although not from any sense of its unimportance. The temptation will be due, rather, to one's sense of frustration over

[22]This thesis is interestingly developed by Raymond Brown in *The Community of the Beloved Disciple* (New York: Paulist Press, 1979).

how and how much can be communicated without confusing the hearers, because these eighteen verses are unusually rich and complex. Categories of understanding familiar to first-century readers sound foreign and strange to modern ears. The interpreter properly ponders the question, Will this lesson or sermon restore to the hearers a portion of their Bible, or will it further diminish or further remove into "long ago and far away" this primary source of the faith?

The second temptation will be to interpret the prologue in segments. This makes sense because of the complexity of the material, provided one defines the segments in such a way that each retains a kind of integrity. But no piecemeal interpretation of this prologue, however carefully executed, can really do it justice. To understand the portrait of Christ in this Gospel one must engage the prologue whole and entire.

The prologue is the place to begin interpreting because it is the evangelist's intention that the reader move through the Gospel equipped with the perspectives on God, Christ, and the world that are provided by the prologue. In fact, this Gospel could be read as a narrative elaboration of the closing line: "No one has ever seen God; the only Son, who is in the bosom of the Father, he has made him known" (1:18).

Some scholars argue on the basis of theological vocabulary and literary form that 1:1-18 may have been added to this Gospel after the completion of the narrative proper. It is true that Jesus is not referred to as the "Word" (Logos) except in the prologue. However, the meaning conveyed by this title is expressed in practically every sign and discourse subsequently related. As to its literary style, there is some agreement that these verses are in the main hymnic, but with two prose additions about John the Baptist (vv 6-8 and 15). The poetic structure may be sensed, even in English, if one reads through the passages as a whole, omitting the prose additions (v 13 may be another).[23] But even if the Prologue does contain a hymn—and this is very likely—the author has adapted it to express, as he understands it, the significance of Christ's person and work. For this reason the prologue should still be regarded as being integral to the Gospel as a whole. The theological perspective of the hymn in its present form is fully congenial to the remainder of the book.

● Before moving on, a suggestion to the interpreter: after presenting the whole of 1:1-18 in both its movement and overall vision, why not use the rather clear literary units within it as an interpretive structure and vehicle? Verses 1-5 are a distinct strophe or unit. In it the Logos is presented with reference to its relation to God and its relation to creation. Notice that the historical figure Jesus is not yet mentioned (not until v 17). Verses 6-8 and 15 should be discussed separately because they interrupt the hymn proper with polemical statements about John the Baptist. The second hymnic unit consists of vv 9-13. Here we see the Logos at work in the world, establishing as children of God all those who are open to receive the light. And finally, vv 14-18 constitute the testimony of the writer and his community who have experienced this Word. The language shifts from that of description to that of witness, "we" and "us." The author and those who share his faith have experienced the eternal Word dwelling in their midst as Jesus of Nazareth. Through him they have come to know the unseen God, and from him they have received grace abundant, as well as the truth concerning God and the life of the world.

What is this evangelist meaning to say about Jesus when he gives him the title "Word" (Logos)? One thinks immediately of God's creative word by which he spoke everything into existence. "In the beginning" says Genesis; "In the beginning"

---

[23]It was not an uncommon practice to insert one's own comments into quoted material in order to adapt it for one's own use. Paul did this in Phil. 2:5-11 and in Col. 1:15-20.

says John. Both Old and New Testaments affirm creation by the word of God (Ps 33:4-7; Heb 11:3). In Jewish and related cultures the word was regarded as an entity separate from its speaker and with power to effect its purpose (Isa 55:10-11). In the course of time the Word became personified as a mediator between God and the world, one by whom God created, sustained, and communicated with the world. The title "Word" was sometimes used interchangeably with the title "Wisdom" (Sophia), and in some texts Wisdom is personified, as if somehow distinct from God, as one who carries out God's will (see, e.g., Prov chap. 8: Wis chap. 7; Sir chap. 24). Such a concept also had currency outside of Judaism, in Hellenistic religions generally and in some philosophical traditions. Wherever such a concept appears it gives expression to two equally important tenets of healthy religion: God is transcendent, distinct from the world; God is related to and involved in the life of the world. The mediating Word is both a witness to that distance between God and the world and a link between the two.

As an aid to our understanding John 1:1-18, let us focus briefly on one use of Word or Wisdom in a document from the general background of the Fourth Gospel. *The Wisdom of Jesus the Son of Sirach* is a Jewish writing broadly familiar in synagogues and churches of the first century. In this book Wisdom is personified as a being distinct from God and yet the companion of God from the beginning, the agent of God in creating the world, and the means by which God revealed himself. According to Sirach 24, a time came when Wisdom expressed the desire to take up residence on earth. Wisdom soon learned however, that the world was a place of darkness and folly and offered no home for Wisdom. God intervened and prepared a dwelling in the tents of Jacob. Thus, says this writer, Wisdom came to reside in Israel, taking the form of a book, the Book of Moses (24:23). The similarities to John 1:1-18 are striking and instructive. But the Evangelist claims that in a person, not a book; in an historical figure, not the personification of an idea, the eternal Word has pitched its tent among us.

● The writer of this Gospel has chosen a category, an image—the "Word"—familiar to his first readers but rather strange to us, and he has applied it to Jesus in order to make several life-giving affirmations. Perhaps if we express these in language more familiar to our own time, the message of the prologue and of this Gospel can become good news for us.

One may consider, first of all, John's view of "the world." Through the Word, God created it, so it is not by origin or nature evil. "*All things* (the totality of what is) were made through him, and without him was not anything made that was made." To think of salvation as basically escape from this world of people and things is to turn one's back on that which God, through Christ, has created. To have a view of salvation that does not embrace all that God created is too small and partial. John recognizes that there is evil and darkness in the world, but he attributes this to human choice: some have "loved darkness rather than light" (3:19). To find one's life in transient values rather than in the Creator is to be of the world and to live by appearance rather than the truth (7:24).

● Anyone bringing to John a predisposition to equate "worldliness" with certain bad habits (against which some pulpits continually rail) must be careful not to use that definition here. Worldliness can be the idolatrous embrace of that which is otherwise good: family, job, one's health, or even one's church. It is significant that this evangelist understands worldliness to assume its ugliest shapes in the entrenchments of religion. The texts, the places, the persons, the rituals, the traditions of religion were created in order to enable service and praise to the Creator, but they have been perverted into defenses and barricades behind which "God's people" resist, rule, and judge. South America, Africa, and even areas of our own country provide painful illustrations of the struggle for basic human rights and freedom meeting resistance in churches that have uncritically embraced the political and economic structures of power. Thus the world God created has become the locus of sin and death.

But God is for, not against, the world. The Creator is now Redeemer. Since the agent of redemption is the same as the agent of creation (i.e., Jesus Christ), none may claim to be Christian while rejecting responsible participation in the life of the world and its human communities. If Creator and Redeemer are one, the realms of creation and of redemption are co-extensive. Jesus the Word addresses the world in judgment because it has preferred not to know God; he addresses it in grace because the one who created it now comes to call it back to God. This is the judgment of the world—light has come. This is the salvation of the world—light has come. Because the Word is not of the world, it is *able* to bring life; because it is sent in God's love to dwell among us in the world, it is *willing* to do so.

Jesus is the embodiment, the incarnation, the Word or Truth of God. His mission, says this Gospel, is to make God known on earth. The person, the words, and the work of Jesus all have this as their central function. This "from above" perspective on Jesus, not only in the prologue, throughout this Gospel (and so unlike most of the Synoptic material), is integral to the writer's understanding of the meaning of Christ in the world. The purpose of this Gospel is not to present a divine Christ to balance a view of a human Christ. Its purpose is to declare that the writer and his community have experienced in the words and deeds of Jesus the grace and the glory of God. This is the good news of the Fourth Gospel. The fundamental human quest is for God, yet no one has ever seen God. Therefore it is in behalf of all of us that Philip says to Jesus, "Lord, show us the Father, and we shall be satisfied" (14:8). Jesus answers, "He who has seen me has seen the Father" (14:9). Or, as the prologue expresses it, "The only Son who is in the bosom of the Father, he has made him known" (1:18).

John 11:1-44
The Raising of Lazarus

The story of the raising of Lazarus has been selected as representative of the sign narratives on the assumption that since they have so much in common in form and theological thrust, interpretive work on one will have transfer value for the other six. However, it must be acknowledged that in at least two respects this particular sign story is not representative. First, in this story we have what is lacking in the others—statements concerning Jesus' own emotions. He was deeply moved, he was troubled, he wept. The church wants and needs every evidence available of Jesus' identification with the human situation, especially with the time of death and grief. This is the story of a death in a family Jesus loved.[24] Understandably, the church has embraced this passage more closely than the other accounts of Jesus' signs. This does not mean, however, that the church has always understood it or has had no problems with it. For example, that Jesus responded to the urgent word of Lazarus' illness by remaining where he was for two more days (v 6) has not rested gently on the hearts of all believers.

The second respect in which this is not a representative sign story is to be found within the Gospel itself. This sign has to carry more theological freight than the others. Here Jesus performs his seventh and last sign, the end of this dimension of his ministry. Just as the Prologue announced that in him were light and life for the world, the sixth and seventh signs

---

[24]The family reappears in John 12:1-3. Elsewhere, Martha and Mary appear, without Lazarus, in Luke 10:38-42. In Luke, Lazarus is the name of a beggar in a story Jesus told (16:19-31).

concretize that promise. The healing of the man born blind (chap. 9) is the sign that Jesus gives light; the raising of Lazarus is the sign that Jesus gives life. But in addition to being the climactic sign that closes his public ministry, this story also introduces the final phase of Jesus' work; the passion. Indeed, it even participates in the passion narrative by precipitating the death of Jesus (vv 45-53), by offering descriptions of Jesus that are very reminiscent of Gethsemane (vv 31-38), and by telling of Lazarus' being raised in language that moves the reader to think of Jesus' own resurrection (vv 38-44).

Having observed these two distinguishing features of the Lazarus story, one still needs to give attention to the characteristics this sign story has in common with the other six. First, as usual the writer makes it clear that Jesus works according to his own "hour," and not according to the promptings or ugings of others. The sisters want him to rush to Bethany—he tarries two days; the disciples do not want him to go at all—he goes anyway. This characteristic parallels Jesus' severing his action in Cana from his mother's suggestion (2:3-4) and his trip to Jerusalem from his brothers' urging (7:3-10).

Second, the signs are performed, not as acts of compassion, but as occasions of revelation. It is quite possible that the source from which John drew this story included something about Jesus' compassion, but this is not a feature of the story as we now have it. Nor is it a feature of the other sign narratives. For example, when the disciples inquired about the cause of a man's blindness, Jesus, before healing him, said the man was blind "that the works of God might be made manifest in him" (9:3). So here in the passage before us, Jesus responds to the news of Lazarus' illness: "This illness is not unto death; it is for the glory of God, so that the Son of God may be glorified by means of it" (v 4).

● It is extremely important that readers of this Gospel be made aware of this peculiarly Johannine perspective on the miracles. One must constantly remember that these texts are in John, not in Luke, and that John's own theological concerns are powerful and nourishing. One must also realize that the signs in John always point beyond themselves to some truth about God and about life. When one recognizes that a sign has a kind of transparency to faith's eyes, then John's explanation that these signs are to reveal God will be clear and acceptable. In fact, meaning and power and pathos are added rather than subtracted when the writer prefaces the story of Lazarus not only with the explanation that this illness is for the glory of God, but most importantly, "that the Son of God may be glorified by means of it" (v 4). Since "being glorified" (returning to glory) is this Gospel's way of referring to Jesus' death, the reader is advised that the events about to be told will bring about the death of Jesus. The raising of Lazarus points beyond itself.

A third characteristic of the sign stories is the element of misunderstanding that enters into them. We referred earlier to the confusion created by the double meanings of such terms as temple, birth, water, and food. Confusion and the inability to understand characterize some who witness this sign also. Thus, Jesus' comment that Lazarus is asleep and must be awakened is met with the disciples' meaningless talk about sleeping and waking up (vv 11-13). Again, at the tomb of Lazarus, the Jews interpret Jesus' tears with, "See how he loved him!" (v 36). By this time we have learned that in John the responses of "the Jews" are wrong. Therefore, the cause of Jesus' tears was something else. Just as there is temple, and then there is the temple of the soul; just as there is water, and then there is the living water; just as there is sleep, and then there is the sleep of death; so there are tears, and then there are Jesus' tears.

A fourth and final characteristic of sign stories, vital to understanding and interpretation, is their crisis-creating impact. The double meanings of which we have spoken actually represent two realms of value, and the sign creates a situation in which one's world of values is revealed for what it is. A temple of stone or a person's life; which temple is to be protected and preserved? Water from the well or living water; for which does one have an appetite? Eyesight or faith sight; Who is blind, and who can see? And now we have a death scene with the body entombed and the mourners in place. Martha grieves over a lost brother and is consoled with the hope of a final resurrection (vv 21-27), but does she, do the mourners, do the Jews, really want life? The life-giver comes, and the disturbance is so fierce that some of them take counsel to make sure that death, not life, prevails. The disturbing life-giver must die; it is "expedient" (vv 45-53).

Once Jesus arrives in Bethany, the drama unfolds in three scenes, each carrying some of the theological weight of the story. The first scene (vv 17-27) shows Jesus with Martha and provides the central truth of the sign soon to take place. Martha had already expressed her trust in the resurrection at the last day (v 24) when Jesus said to her, "I am the resurrection and the life; he who believes in me, though he die, yet shall he live, and whoever lives and believes in me shall never die" (vv 25-26). Earlier in this Gospel there had been statements on eternal life as a present reality: "He who believes in the Son *has* eternal life" (3:36) and "He who hears my word and believes him who sent me, *has* eternal life; he does not come into judgment, but *has passed* from death to life" (5:24). Here again the message is clear: eternal life begins, not at the funeral home and not at the end of time, but with him. Whoever believes in him has life. Death will come, but not the death that separates from God. Physical death is robbed of its power and threat because in Christ there is life on both sides of the grave. In fact, the one who trusts lives as though death were a past, not a future experience.

It must be acknowledged that this Gospel emphasizes the presence now of eternal life. This may be a reaction to an overemphasis by some early Christians on future fulfillment, future life, and a general postponement of blessedness until this life and this world are gone. We cannot be sure. In any case, John's emphasis on eternal life *now* certainly does function as a corrective. John says "Every day," not "Someday," is the believer's experience of life. However, this Gospel does not eliminate the future dimension of eternal life. "Though he die, yet shall he live" refers to the future, as do 5:21 and 14:1-3. This writer has not chosen present instead of future, he has only underscored the importance of the present. Interpreters sometimes lay hold of the Fourth Gospel's *today* and fail to mention its *tomorrow*.

The second scene (vv 28-37) involves Jesus and Mary in the midst of the mourners. Whereas the earlier sketch of Jesus with Martha provided the truth statement about Jesus as the one who gives life, with Mary and the mourners Jesus is portrayed in his emotional response to all that is going on around him and to the act about to be performed. It is only a teasing guess that the sequence of the scenes with Martha and Mary and the difference in Jesus' response to each of them represents a knowledge of Luke's story of the two women (Luke 10:38-42).

The moment of the sign is near, and the scene is difficult to interpret for several reasons. Here the interpreter deals not with Jesus' words and deeds but with his emotions. No other stories in John provide anything similar. In this Gospel, Gethsemane holds no agonizing struggle; Jesus seems to be in complete control during betrayal, arrest, and trial, and his death is without screams. As he had said, he laid down his life, no one took it from him (10:18). Only here in chapter 11 is it said: "deeply moved in spirit and troubled"; "Jesus wept"; "deeply moved again" (vv 33-38).

The commentaries will provide a number of meanings for the words used here: disturbed, chafed, angry, moved as with pity, upset, agitated. It seems safe to rule out the usual emotional response at the funeral of a friend. Jesus has moved too deliberately for that; he knows this occasion is not one of new life for a friend but of new life for the world. The immediate human relationships, as in all the sign stories, are transcended by the truth about to be revealed. And besides, this is the interpretation given Jesus' emotions by those who always misunderstand. Then should we interpret Jesus' weeping here as anger, as some hold? Is he disturbed because of this display of unbelief, a crowd draped in black and shaking in grief (some of it manufactured by the professional mourners), while in their midst is the one who is himself the resurrection and the life? (Quite possibly.)

But the interpreter may also wish to consider reading the scene as this Gospel's Gethsemane. Since there is no struggle later, on the night of his arrest (18:1-12), perhaps the struggle is here. Certainly Jesus' emotions are not responding simply to the conditions of the moment. That Jesus is moved here, but not at the sight of hungry multitudes (6:1-6) or of a palsied man (5:1-9) or of one born blind (9:1-4) can hardly be explained by saying, "But these were his friends." Jesus is moved by what is *really* taking place: "This illness is not unto death; it is for the glory of God, so that the Son of God may be glorified by means of it" (v 4). What is really happening is that Jesus is about to perform the act that will bring about his own death (vv 45-53). Notice that when he approaches the tomb he is deeply moved again; to call Lazarus out is to put himself in. The expression "being troubled" occurs again at 12:27: "Now is my soul troubled. And what shall I say, 'Father, save me from this hour'?" "This hour" is the hour of death. In chap. 11, the sign is performed which precipitated that hour, and in chap. 12 there is a discourse reflecting on its meaning. The hour has been embraced; all that remains is death itself, triumphant and without tears.

The third and final scene is the sign itself (vv 38-44). The dramatic elements are briefly but powerfully sketched. His command to remove the stone is met with Martha's remonstrance: Please, it has been four days and the body is already decaying; there will be an odor. He calls on her to trust, and the stone is removed (vv 38-41*a*). There follows the prayer (vv 41*b*-42), the loud cry to Lazarus (v 43), and the command, "Unbind him, and let him go" (v 44). Then it is over. But when the drama of it has released its grip, what has been read? All the signals are here: the cave tomb, the stone rolled away, the prayer, the loud scream, the grave clothes. Who can read this and not have the mind shift from Lazarus to Jesus' death, burial, and resurrection? Surely the writer had this in mind. This is a sign, and beyond what is apparently happening is what is really happening. It is as though one held up to the light a sheet of paper on which was written the story of the raising of Lazarus. But bleeding through from the reverse side of the paper, and clear enough to be read, is the other story of the death and resurrection of Jesus.

● Perhaps the comments on one or more of the three scenes in the dramatic story have already prompted the interpreter toward a lesson or sermon. Even so, one theme in scene one is too important not to be repeated. Jesus said, "I am the resurrection and the life," not only as a promise, but as a *correction* to Martha's faith. She believed in a resurrection at the last day, in eternal life totally in the future. Jesus offers her more, not less; he offers life eternal now and in the future. His offer needs to be repeated to all those whose present is barren, but who try to survive on a distant hope. Regrettably, one often hears Jesus' words recited at funerals with an interpretation that reveals only Martha's faith.

A final word to the interpreter: reflect upon the form of this passage. A story of a death in a family is told as a narrative about Jesus' own passion, and Jesus' own passion is told as a narrative about a death in a family. When anyone's story and Jesus' story are so interwoven, it is not simply a literary display; it is a presentation of the gospel.

John 14–16
Farewell and Promise

One of the most striking features of the Gospel of John is the amount of attention given to Jesus and his disciples after the close of Jesus' public ministry. The ministry of signs and the revelation discourses end at 12:50, with nine chapters yet remaining. One would suppose at first that John has simply expanded the narrative of Jesus' arrest, trial, crucifixion, and resurrection. Such is not the case, however. That narrative is remarkably similar to the one in the Synoptics. The additional volume of material consists primarily of discourses and a prayer of Jesus. The governing mood here is one of farewell.

Why so much farewell? There is a farewell meal, a lengthy discourse (or discourses), and a farewell prayer prior to the actual departure. In this long, and at times repetitious, section the writer seems to be giving attention to the major crisis of the early church: the absence of Jesus. Jesus departs to go to the Father and leaves the disciples (the church) in the world. Now what are they to do? Is it over? Do they return to Galilee and their fishing boats? If not, where do they go, and who is in charge? Just what does the church do after Easter? Can the church survive on its memory of things said and done by Jesus?

● John is not alone among the Gospel writers in this concern. As we have seen, Mark comes abruptly to an end without a single resurrection appearance, but he does offer at least one promise to the disciples left behind: Jesus will meet you in Galilee (16:7). Matthew shows that the promised meeting actually took place, and adds another promise: "I am with you always" (28:20). Luke takes a different turn. The risen Christ commands the disciples to remain in Jerusalem until they receive the Holy Spirit (24:49), and The Book of Acts is the account of receiving and living out the presence of that Spirit.

The Fourth Evangelist deals with the absence of Jesus in a different way, although there are some similarities in his approach with Luke's emphasis on the gift of the spirit. In a farewell address (chaps. 14–17), Jesus tells his disciples what they can expect in the world and what their life as a faith community is to be. He assures them that everything they will need for life and mission in the world will be provided. Even though this is presented as an address by the historical Jesus, it is best interpreted as the living Christ speaking to the Johannine church about its own situation.

The farewell address was a familiar literary type in the ancient world, both in and outside the Bible. In the Old Testament, farewell speeches by Jacob, Moses, and Joshua serve to gather up and interpret a community's past, present, and future; and in the New Testament, Paul's farewell speech to the Ephesian elders functions in the same way (Acts 20:17-35). Many commentators believe we should not think of chaps. 14–16 of John as a single farewell address. They point out, for example, that 14:31 seems to end a discourse which, in fact, continues (15:1ff.). And 16:5 ("None of you asks me, 'Where are you going?'") seems unaware of 13:36 ("Simon Peter said to him, 'Lord, where are you going?'"). Doubtless, the seams still show after the writer has put his sources and his own material together. Nevertheless, we can without violence to intention treat these three chapters as a single farewell discourse. It has been given a formal ending in 16:33.

● Once the interpreter has gotten in mind the form, scope, intent, and overall theological achievement of this discourse, it is legitimate to probe for vital centers of meaning. That is what we will seek to do here.

Basically what Christ says to the church in this passage is: (a) I have finished my work on earth, and I am returning to my Father and the glory I had before coming into the world, but (b) I will not leave you to fend for yourselves as orphans in this world. The importance of the glorification of the Son and his return to the Father should not be minimized, but the weight of the discourse falls on the promise to the church to whom Jesus is saying farewell. With the passing of time, the absence of Christ has grown ever more critical, and the discourse is addressed chiefly to this problem.

The central content of the promise to the church is that Christ (and the Father) will send the Holy Spirit, the Spirit of Truth, referred to here in the first instance with the term peculiar to the Johannine community, the "Paraclete" (14:16, 26; 15:26; 16:7).[25] Although there are implied references throughout this section, the specific sayings concerning the Spirit come in 14:16-17, 25-26; 15:26; 16:7-10, 12-15. Given some repetition in these passages, the following can be said in summary.

1. Christ asks the Father to send to his church one to replace him, another helper or advocate, who will never leave, but who will be with the church forever.

2. The Spirit will teach the church, will guide it in the truth, and will speak concerning what is yet to be.

3. The Spirit will remind the church of what Jesus said.

4. The Spirit will not witness to himself, but to Christ; he will not glorify himself, but only Christ; he will not speak on his own authority, but will speak only what Christ gives him to speak.

[25]"Paraclete" is a transliteration of a Greek word, the verb form of which means "to call alongside," apparently for aid or comfort. Check several English versions for different translations of the word.

5. The Spirit, in addition to his ministry to the church, will convince and convict the world of its errors.

How are we to interpret these sayings about the Holy Spirit in the life of the church? Given the continuing tension in the church between "charismatics" and those who listen more carefully to tradition and structure, we bring more than historical interest to this farewell discourse.

The church, says this Gospel, is to be open to the guidance of the Holy Spirit. However, John is not unaware of the dangers implicit in "the leading of the Spirit." Without canons for testing the "spirit," confusion and division can follow. John's own community, or else some groups nearby, apparently suffers from the presence of spirit-led prophets who are in radical discontinuity with the tradition. Therefore stern and repeated warnings are sounded: the Spirit will not witness to himself, will not glorify himself, will not speak on his own. One criterion is given for testing any claim for speaking in the Spirit: Is the message in clear continuity with the word of the historical Jesus? The Holy Spirit brings to remembrance the teachings of Jesus and says what is in accord with what he said. The church, therefore, is to resist discontinuity even when it is flying the banner of the Spirit. John's community claimed this continuity with Jesus as the true sign of the Spirit's presence and found the continuity completely in accord with the apostolic source the community claimed for its tradition (19:35; 21:24). But the church cannot be locked into the past; the Spirit leads into new truth. This, too, vibrates with dangers, but John is unwilling to be frightened into closure, thereby quenching the Spirit and forbidding prophecy, as did the church at Thessalonica (1 Thess 5:19-20).

The Paraclete sayings and, in fact, the entire farewell discourse, make it abundantly clear that for John the work of the Holy Spirit is primarily witnessing. The spirit, like Jesus, will have a ministry of the Word. Jesus' revelation of God came primarily in words, in discourses. The community is a community of the Word. To be sure, Jesus performed miracles (signs), and the church is told it will do even greater works (14:12), but both in Jesus' ministry and in his discourse to the church, such activity is clearly subordinate to his speaking the Word.

● In view of the widespread interest in the Holy Spirit and of the unusual amount of attention given to Paul's discussion in First Corinthians 12–14, the interpreter would do well to share in some detail John's teaching here. Such sermons or lessons need not be offered to counter those who focus entirely on First Corinthians, but to enlarge understanding and appreciation of this rich and complex subject. It is helpful to see the varieties of ways in which the New Testament reflects the church's experience of the Spirit and its struggle to identify clear evidence of the Spirit's presence. This attention to John's discussion of the Holy Spirit could also be an occasion for illustrating the importance of respecting the integrity of each writer when doing Bible study. John and Paul are not the same, nor did they write to the same church.

It is possible that the Fourth Gospel is itself a product of the community's Spirit-led prophetic ministry. But whatever may have been the self-understanding of the person or persons involved in its composition, what is very important to remember is that this prophetic work (what the living Christ is saying to the church) is in the form of a Gospel, that it is a presentation of the ministry of Jesus of Nazareth. John is absolutely certain on this point: any spirit that would sever the good news from history, from Jesus in the flesh, is not the Holy Spirit.

● Lessons or sermons on this section of John could be both informed and enlivened by material from an early Christian document called *The Didache: The Teaching of the Twelve Apostles.* It can be found in a volume entitled *The Apostolic Fathers.* In *The Didache,* chaps. 11–13, there is a most interesting discussion of how the church can determine if one who claims to have the Holy Spirit actually does. By means of this document, a church today might be stimulated to clarify its own thinking on the subject.

One other question arises inevitably in the study of this farewell discourse: Does this writer regard the promise of the Spirit's coming to the church as, in fact, the promise of Christ's own return at the Parousia? Out of the content of this section, two responses can be made. First, John undoubtedly places much more emphasis on the present realization of eternal life than on eternal life as a hope for the future. We have noted this already, but we have also reminded ourselves that in the Gospel as we now have it, this accent on the present has not removed the future dimension. The future is definitely a part of the disciple's life of faith in this discourse (e.g., 14:3). Whether this future clause served primarily as a guard against those forms of Christian experience that collapse the whole of faith into one present moment is not certain. The fact remains that the word about the future of the believer's relation to Christ is still in this Gospel.

The second response is that this mixture of present and future adds to the ambiguity of the writer's identifying and not identifying Christ's coming and the Spirit's coming. As we have seen, in these texts Christ and the Holy Spirit are distinctly different: Christ will send the Spirit; the Spirit will be *another* Helper. Yet it is possible to read some lines as identification of the two. "I will not leave you desolate; I will come to you. Yet a little while, and the world will see me no more, but you will see me; because I live, you will live also. In that day you will know that I am in my Father, and you in me, and I in you" (14:18-20). Or again, "If a man loves me, he will keep my word, and my

Father will love him, and *we* will come to him and make *our* home with him" (14:23). Does this first personal plural include Father and Son or Father, Son, and Holy Spirit? Obviously, the language to describe the Divine Presence in the Christian community has not yet hardened into trinitarian formulas that respect three persons in one God. Rather, the expressions seem more fluid, more functional, more experiential. There is no concern to distinguish "God with us" from "Christ with us" or "the Spirit with us." It may also be helpful to remind ourselves that John does not use the expression "second coming," as though there were only the one "coming" as the historical Jesus and the second as the triumphant Christ. More appropriate to the discourse would be the observation that Christ comes to his church: he comes following his resurrection, he comes as indwelling, he comes as Holy Spirit, he comes at last to receive the church to himself.

John 19:31-37
The Witness of the Corpse

● This paragraph lies within John's passion narrative, yet of all the units within that narrative, it may seem to be the least important. It is preceded by the accounts of the betrayal, arrest, trial, and crucifixion, and it is followed by the stories of the burial and resurrection. But these verses deal only with the treatment of the bodies, one of them already lifeless, as they hang on the crosses. Even the creedal summaries—crucified, dead, and buried—give not a word to the event of this paragraph. If a reader of this text regards these verses as conveying information, then that holds some satisfaction because followers of Jesus have only scant historical data about him, in life or in death. Any word or line is hungrily received. But that obviously is not the writer's intent, whatever may have been the form and nature of his source.

We give attention to this text because the Gospel writer has forced the reader to pause and reflect on the significance of the treatment of Jesus' corpse. Having observed that the side of Jesus was pierced by a soldier's spear, causing blood and water to come out, the writer comments editorially: "He who saw it has borne witness—his testimony is true, and he knows that he tells the truth—that you also may believe" (v 35). What a strange thing to say! What has been said that is so important, so controversial, so central to the writer's purpose, that he would interrupt the narrative to attest to the reliability of the witness? And what is "the truth" the readers are supposed to believe? If the passage is so significant for this writer, then it deserves some special attention.

In this text we engage, as clearly as in any passage in John, the delight and the burden of interpreting this Gospel. With his double meanings, two-level drama, events as signs, and words that convey the Word, this writer invites probing beneath the surface of things, teases into theological speculation, and demands symbolic interpretations. In other words, those "too imaginative" approaches to texts about which we are properly warned when exploring most areas of Scripture are here called back into service. The reason is not that any method is permitted when encountering baffling texts, but that John himself builds in so much symbolism that being true to the text requires such quests for meaning. Here as elsewhere the interpreter must not only be guided, but also limited, by the writer, lest profundity be sought beneath every word and "found" where it was never intended.

But therein lies the difficulty. What and where are the restraints upon a spiritualizing imagination when dealing with this brief account? Where and how may we find in this story—which is present in no other Gospel—a significant word of Christian witness? Some of the early church fathers apparently felt more permission than restraint in their interpretations. For example, some claimed that just as Adam's bride came forth from his side, so out of the side of Christ came his bride, the church. Or, as Eve came from Adam's side, and through Eve came sin, so from the side of the second Adam came atonement for sin. Or again, as blood and water came from Christ's side, so are his followers to submit to two baptisms, water and martyrdom. Far-fetched interpretations such as these should drive us back to the text itself, to see what is really intended.

On the day of Jesus' death two systems clash. Although they had collaborated on the killing of Jesus, now the Romans and the Jews differ on the disposal of bodies. The Romans often left the body of a criminal on display as a deterrent to crime, but Jewish law forbade a body to be left hanging overnight (Deut 21:22-23; Josh 8:29). This would have been of special concern at the time of Jesus' crucifixion since the next day was a high sabbath, the beginning of Passover (v 31). So the Jews suggested Roman justice would be served by the *crurifragium*, breaking the legs with a heavy mallet to prevent possible escape and to suffocate the victims, and then taking the bodies down. It was agreed, and the two thieves were so treated (v 32). But Jesus was already dead (v 33). Perhaps as a check to be sure, a spear was thrust into his side, and out came blood and water (v 34). These things, says John, fulfilled two scriptures, Exodus 12:46 (Num 9:12) and Zechariah 12:10.

In a sense yet to be explored, this account of what happened is not simply a witnesses' account of what took place. It is the Christian witness of one who understood its meaning and is seeking to generate faith. In each of the Gospels, the account of Jesus' death is followed at once by testimonies of faith: the confession of the soldier, the splitting of the temple curtain, the dead leaving their tombs (Matt 27:51-54; Mark 15:38-39; Luke 23:44-49). All of these testimonies underscore the transcendent importance of what has just taken place. Simply to record Jesus' dying would hardly be a Gospel and would certainly not qualify as a word of witness. That the Messiah of God, the Lord of the church, was executed by the Romans, was the major burden upon all efforts of that church to preach and claim disciples. Therefore the word that needed desperately to be said was not just that he died, but that his dying had purpose and meaning in the plan of God and for the life of the world. None of the Synoptic testimonies to the ultimate importance of Jesus' death is found in John. In their stead is the witness of 19:31-37. What is the particular import of this witness, this truth given that the reader may believe?

Some interpreters believe that the main point in these verses is that Jesus really did die. Such a view regards the paragraph as being directed at a heretical group referred to as "Docetics." The Docetics held such a lofty view of Christ's divinity that they had to conclude he only seemed to be a human in the flesh and only seemed to die. This position apparently was held by some in the Johannine circle itself, because First John devotes a great deal of attention to those anti-Christs who deny Jesus has come in the flesh (4:1-6). In fact, this kind of spiritualization of the Gospel became such a threat to the church that the early creeds sought to counter it by emphasizing that Jesus really was "crucified, dead, and buried." But it is unlikely that the purpose of the passage before us was exclusively polemical, as appropriate as that would have been.

Other interpreters believe that this text is John's symbolic presentation of the Synoptic account of the tearing of the temple veil. According to this view, the clue is provided by 2:21 where the Evangelist interprets Jesus' reference to the temple as a reference to his own body. Therefore here, it is suggested, the lance in his side represents the splitting of the temple veil. However, this view accentuates the spear thrust, whereas it is the outpouring of blood and water that seems to be the focus of the writer's attention. This passage does indeed help to make the point that Jesus' death brought an end to the temple cult, but it makes this point in another way, as we shall see.

It is very difficult to interprét symbolic language, and one's conclusions should always be cautious and tentative. With this appropriate hesitation, two ideas may be ventured about John 19:31-37. First, the specific reference to blood and water most likely points to the sacraments of eucharist and baptism. The sacraments of the church are directly related to the death of Jesus, just as is the giving of the Holy Spirit (7:38-39).[26] Many readers of this Gospel have been struck by the writer's extensive use of water, wine, blood, and bread in the stories about Jesus, and it seems fair to conclude that in many if not all of these stories the writer had in mind the sacraments of the church. In some places this is obvious, as in the eucharistic discourse of 6:35-59. Equally clear is the sacramental reference in the word to Nicodemus about being "born of water and the Spirit" (3:5). Some believe that there are similar meanings buried in the story of Jesus' changing water to wine (2:1-11) and in the conversation at Jacob's well (4:7-15).

Second, it would appear that John wishes to interpret the death of Jesus as bringing an end to the Jewish cultus. The end of that cultus is not by pronouncement or abrogation but by fulfillment. Not only in 19:31-37, but in the entire passion narrative, one notices many references to the fulfillment of Scripture. True, there have been allusions to and citations of Old Testament texts throughout this Gospel. But now in the passion narrative the Scripture not only bears witness, but is fulfilled. Whether these Scripture citations appeared in the narrative as John received it or are Johannine in origin, as they

---

[26]1 John 5:6-8 combines blood, water, and spirit as witnesses to Christ. It is generally agreed 1 John comes from the same community that produced this Gospel.

now stand they declare that Jesus' death did not in any way negate or put the lie to all that he had said and done. On the contrary, not only were the details of his death prophesied in Scripture, but his death actually brought to completion what had only been anticipated in Israel's word and ritual.

In particular, the death of Jesus is here understood to have fulfilled the central event of Israel's history, the Exodus. Jesus is presented as the Passover lamb. Unlike the Synoptic accounts, John places Jesus' death on the day before Passover, the very day the Passover lamb was slaughtered. The evangelist's concern here is probably more theological than chronological. The symbolism is obvious: on the very afternoon that the blood of the Passover lambs was drained from their bodies, blood poured out from Jesus' side; as the lambs were slaughtered without breaking bones, so not a single bone of Jesus' body was broken (vv 33, 36). As the Passover lamb, Jesus' death launches a New Exodus for all who believe; he enables their release from the darkness, sin, and death of the world.

● The interpreter will want to be careful here lest listeners confuse the symbolism of the Passover lamb with that of the lamb slain as a sacrifice for sin. Jesus as the sacrifice for sin is a theme developed in Hebrews against the backdrop of Jewish ritual, and occurs as a minor note in Pauline thought (Rom 3:21-26). But this passage in John is entirely different. Here we do not meet Jesus in atoning death but in liberating death. The Passover lamb was the symbol of freedom from slavery and of the quest for the promised land. Interpretations of the death of Jesus in this Gospel should not, therefore, become entangled in theories of atonement and expiation from sin. Rather, one's interpretation should call upon the rich images of Exodus, of liberation, of freedom in the knowledge of God. The truth, says John, sets free (8:32).

It would not be at all out of order for the interpreter to tie together the two principal thoughts which have emerged here in

19:31-37: the symbolism of the sacraments of baptism and the eucharist and the symbolism of Exodus and the Passover. Both baptism and the eucharist bear the liberation themes well. In fact, the Synoptics present the baptism of Jesus within the Exodus motif (Mark 1:2-13 and parallels), and they interpret the last supper of Jesus as both a Passover meal and as the Christian eucharist (Mark 14:12-25 and parallels). Moreover, Paul, interpreting the Exodus typologically, speaks of the Red Sea crossing as a baptismal experience and of the food and drink in the wilderness as a kind of eucharist (1 Cor 10:1-4). The interpreter, therefore, would not only be well within the meaning of John 19:31-37, but also supported by other New Testament writers, in presenting the sacraments as the rituals of a New Exodus and the gospel as a proclamation of freedom.

CONCLUSION: TO BE CONTINUED

We began this discussion with comments about interpreting in general, interpreting scripture in particular, and interpreting the Gospels specifically. We reminded ourselves that interpreting goes on all the time as a part of negotiating life, privately and communally. The task increases in difficulty if that which is to be interpreted is extremely important and especially if it is distant from us in terms of time, place, language, and related considerations.

Understandably, the interpreter of scripture feels the burden of this difficulty, but is not discouraged. On the contrary, our common humanity, the continuity of the community which has preserved and interpreted the sacred texts, and the presence of scholars who serve that community by ceaseless investigations of those texts, are facts which combine to make interpreting scripture not only possible but fruitful.

This book has sought to encourage the participation of the readers, especially preachers and teachers, in the process of interpreting biblical texts. This attempt has been in the form of suggesting some procedural guidelines and then applying them in the exploration of selected texts from the Gospels. The reader is now urged to continue the process by following the Guidelines into other texts in the Gospels.

Interpretation is never final and complete. It is the interpreter's task to effect in every time and place a new hearing of the Word of God.

AIDS FOR THE INTERPRETER

A small library of basic resources is indispensable in the task of interpreting Scripture, whether for oneself or for lessons and sermons. These books and periodicals are colleagues; supporting, correcting, and clarifying one's own lifelong engagement with the text itself. The following are recommended as proven friends of the interpreter of the Gospels.

General Works

The New Oxford Annotated Bible with the Apocrypha. New York: Oxford University Press, 1973. A good study Bible is basic. A wealth of helpful articles and notes.

Clinton Morrison, *An Analytical Concordance to the Revised Standard Version of the New Testament.* Philadelphia: The Westminster Press, 1979. Saves hours of searching and makes one confident as to thoroughness in references to appropriate texts.

Interpreter's Dictionary of the Bible. 5 vols. Nashville: Abingdon, 1962, 1976. Will do the work of fifty books. Treats every significant person, place, event, topic.

Gospel Parallels. New York: Thomas Nelson, 1967. Matthew, Mark, Luke in parallel columns, giving immediate access to all three, and making vivid and inescapable certain issues central to Gospel study. Appropriate references to John in footnotes.

Commentaries

Paul Achtemeier, *Mark* (Proclamation Commentaries Series). Philadelphia: Fortress Press, 1975. Good brief overview, with preacher in mind.

E. Schweizer, *The Good News According to Mark.* trans. Donald Madvig. Richmond: John Knox, 1970. Comments on the text, unit by unit.

J. D. Kingsbury, *Matthew* (Proclamation Commentaries Series). Philadelphia: Fortress Press, 1977. Good sketch of structure and theology of Matthew for teacher, preacher.

E. Schweizer, *The Good News According to Matthew.* trans. D. E. Green. Atlanta: John Knox, 1975. Same format as commentary on Mark.

E. E. Ellis, *The Gospel of Luke.* Greenwood, S. C.: Attic Press, 1974. Excellent introduction to Luke and scholarly work without being too technical.

F. W. Danker, *Jesus and the New Age: According to St. Luke.* St. Louis: Clayton Publishing House, 1974. Offers different views of the familiar. Use along with another commentary.

Raymond Brown, *The Gospel According to John.* 2 vols. Garden City, New York: Doubleday, 1966, 1970. The best, most complete commentary on John.

D. M. Smith, *John* (Proclamation Commentaries Series). Philadelphia: Fortress Press, 1976. Clear, concise statement on structure and theology of John.

Special Studies

W. D. Davies, *The Sermon on the Mount.* London: Cambridge University Press, 1966.

J. Jeremias, *The Parables of Jesus.* New York: Scribners, 1972 (2nd rev. ed.).

F. W. Beare, *The Earliest Records of Jesus.* New York: Abingdon, 1962. Companion to *Gospel Parallels;* comments on form and literary history of each unit.

H. Conzelmann, *The Theology of St. Luke.* trans. Geoffrey Buswell. New York: Harper & Row, 1961. At times difficult but a landmark study of Luke's theological perspective.

Robert Kysar, *John, The Maverick Gospel.* Atlanta: John Knox, 1976. Brief, readable, designed for one beginning a study of John.

L. E. Keck, *The Bible in the Pulpit.* Nashville: Abingdon, 1978. Excellent discussion (with three examples) of use of good biblical interpretation in preaching. Can apply as well to teaching.

Periodical

Interpretation. Richmond: Union Theological Seminary. A quarterly which works consistently at relating biblical studies to the teaching and preaching of the church.

3 5282 00727 0344